Dating After Trauma

"Through this courageous display of vulnerability Emily details how to move past a traumatic experience and live an empowered and fulfilled life rather than living as a victim. The feelings expressed in this story will resonate with anyone who as ever experienced any form of trauma. The advice will provide valuable skills you can use for the rest of your life."

--Michelle Westling

"Emily uses her personal experiences, insights about herself and valuable wisdom to offer hope and healing for women who have struggled with sexual abuse, PTSD, and unhealthy dating relationships. She is able to articulate what she has gained through her healing process in a way that the reader can gain their own insights on how to develop healthy coping skills and a heightened sense of self-respect, discernment in choosing safe partners, and establishing boundaries. I would strongly recommend this book for anyone who feels stuck in the present due to past abusive relationships or trauma."

--Jennifer Wu, Licensed Clinical Social Worker

"Emily couples her authentic voice and compassion to produce a practical, no-nonsense guide to finding healthy love after trauma. As someone who hasn't experienced trauma in dating relationships, I was surprised that much of her guidance resonated deeply with me. I also gained new insight into how to be supportive to those in my life that have experienced dating trauma. Reading this book will feel like your best girlfriend is walking you through the challenges of healing after dating trauma, so you can prepare yourself for the healthy relationship you deserve!"

--Mary Francis, Ph.D.

DATING

After

TRAUMA

How to find the love of your life after experiencing an abusive relationship, rape, or sexual abuse

Emily Avagliano

Dating *After* Trauma

Printed in the United States of America

ISBN-13: 978-0615850061 (Bad Kitty Print Shoppe)

Learn more information at:

www.datingaftertrauma.com

Dedication

I would like to dedicate this book to my therapist, Jennifer, who taught me how to take down the wall of fear, trust myself, and love again.

Also, to my husband, Aaron. You are my rock of strength. I never imagined a love so meaningful and satisfying in my life. I am at peace at your side.

And to my parents, thank you for being there in the best and worst of times.

Table of Contents

List of Tables

Introduction

On May 26, 2012, I married the man of my dreams on the beautiful Hawaiian Island of Kauai. It was at sunset on the beach at the gorgeous St. Regis Resort. Surrounded by my closest friends and family, we said our vows, and I realized how far I had come in my emotional development from the first day of my sexual trauma. My husband is my closest friend, passionate lover, and the ultimate litmus test of my healing. I want this bliss for you!

Before I met and ultimately married Aaron, several events occurred in my life that damaged my self-esteem and made me question if I would ever get married. From early dating experiences in high school and college where boundaries were not honored, to sexual harassment at work, to a massage therapist touching me inappropriately, I unfortunately have a wealth of knowledge when it comes to sexual confusion and abuse. It took me many years to heal from these incidents and find love.

I am not a psychologist or therapist, nor have I been formally trained in healing those who have suffered a major trauma or psychological illness.

This book is based on my own personal story of how I healed myself from pain, regained my self-esteem, and had the courage to date again to fulfill my deepest desire to fall in love, get married, and start a family.

Unlike books on the market today that address the near-term healing from abusive relationships or sexual abuse, this book is about moving on from the pain and regaining your love life. I will examine common, destructive patterns of behavior and mental filtering that often prevent you from reaching your goal of falling in love with a good person. It is not the actual event that is causing you pain, but rather the meaning you are assigning to it that is preventing you from moving forward. It is what you are telling yourself in your head about yourself and your ability to find love that we will together deconstruct and fix.

I would recommend this book to anyone who has suffered from an attack or abusive boyfriend, anyone dating a person who has experienced trauma, or a parent or friend who wants to understand how to help. This book will uncover common patterns in your thoughts and actions that may be preventing you from finding love. I will also provide a methodology of how to successfully date and find love, based on my own experience.

After suffering a sexual trauma or abuse, it takes tremendous courage to date. It is even more difficult to accept intimacy from a good person. However, once you know what to look for in terms of roadblocks, the path to love becomes much easier.

I wish you tremendous success in your love life. Please send me an e-mail and let me know what you have discovered. The website is www.datingaftertrauma.com.

Chapter 1: Trauma and the Day After

I went through a series of painful events in my life that lead me to a dark period of sadness and depression. Some events were mild, more like a "misunderstanding" between me and a boyfriend in my high school and early college days. When I entered the workforce, I was approached sexually by superiors and customers twice my age. I had difficulty keeping up with my sexuality, as if I were broadcasting, "Hey weirdo, come bother me." I did not know how to turn off my sexuality and felt incredibly frustrated. I often felt humiliated by the fact that this just kept happening to me. I was so high strung, always on guard for the next attack. How can someone become a magnet for abuse and pain?

In my early thirties, my parents felt so badly for me that they took me to a resort in central Texas to try to help me to relax. Unfortunately, during a massage, I was sexually abused. I remember lying there motionless, unable to actually conceive it was happening. It was as if time had stopped and everything was moving through water. I had let my guard down, relaxed for one moment, and this is what happened. Did I want this? Seconds earlier, I was enjoying a hot stone massage, and now someone was touching me. Did I do something to make him think I wanted this? What should I do? I had a rock in my hand and I imagined bludgeoning the man to death. Instead, I slowly sat up on the table and cried.

He kept saying, "It is ok. This is just part of the massage." He put his hand on my back to comfort me. This is the worst part of abuse: mixed, confusing messages from your attacker and weird thoughts in your head about who to blame. After such a violent act, the man is comforting me and telling me I read it incorrectly. Did this man really think he was pleasing me? Did I do something to indicate I wanted a "happy ending"? The worst is your body sexually playing tricks on you, mixing up pleasure, fear, pain, and terror. Did I enjoy the massage too much? Did I enjoy the abuse sexually? If I blame myself, do I not have to face the horrific pain of knowing I failed to protect myself yet again? Does blaming myself give me the opportunity to control the situation?

I ran from the massage table wrapped in the blanket toward the women's locker room. I locked myself in the bathroom. It was late. I had scheduled the massage right before dinner with my parents, and the spa was closing down. I wept loudly, alone, unable to move.

The lady from the counter appeared, telling me the spa was closing down, and I had to pay. She noticed I was crying and asked what was wrong. I could not form a sentence. I stayed in that bathroom for twenty more minutes, crying. Finally, the woman convinced me to come out and pay.

I remember handing her my credit card. At this point, I just wanted to get back to my hotel room as fast as possible. I remember looking down at the credit card receipt at the line where you are supposed to enter a tip. How fucked-up is this! I was so angry, but I wanted to leave. I drew a line through it, signed my name, and ran.

When I got back to the room, my mother was standing there, asking why I was late. "We are going to miss our dinner reservation and your dad has already gone to the restaurant to hold our table." I just sobbed loudly and ran to the shower. Intellectually, I knew I was not supposed to do this, as it would destroy evidence, but nothing on earth could stop me from showering. I washed so hard my arms were red with nail marks.   I was trying to get the event off of me. Erase it. Get it away from me.

My mom came into the bathroom. "What's wrong? You are scaring me. Are you ok?" I just kept crying. She was right to be scared. This was a very dangerous time for me. Suicide was an option I was considering as a way to make it stop. Instead, I kept on scrubbing.

Finally, I broke down and told my mom what had happened. Now she was in shock. She could not fathom what had happened and wanted it to go away just as badly as I did. "Let's go to dinner and talk it over with your Dad."

"What? Go out in public? Are you crazy? I want to stay here." Slowly, she convinced me this was the right thing to do, but inside I felt betrayed. Why had my parents failed to protect me? The only way to describe how I felt was as if I had been dropped in a war zone and everything felt like life and death. The idea of eating food in such a moment of serious crisis made it feel like my mother was blind to the tank coming over the hill with its bazooka aimed directly at our hotel room. We were in two different worlds.

As we walked to the restaurant, I tried to swallow my feelings. I breathed slowly, and my crying was a slow sigh. Forget about it and eat dinner. This never happened. The whole reason I came on this trip was to let go of past events, and now this was so much more horrifying then any of the last. Things were escalating, and I had no idea how to stop them.

We sat at the table. I tried not to cry, but my dad immediately noticed my red face. "What's wrong?"

Everything was still moving in water, in slow motion. I looked around for the next attack, thinking that the normalcy of eating dinner was so out of place with my horrifying thoughts. Fear overwhelmed me. Slowly, I told my dad what happened, and he immediately went into action to protect me.

"We are leaving here now!" my dad said with anger. Finally, someone showed the proper emotion to an attack.

My mother, still in shock, said, "Do you want to eat dinner first?"

"No! We are going home."

We packed our clothes and drove home that night. My dad got the hotel to refund our money, including the massage. I felt good about that. My dad also told me the hotel fired the massage therapist, but that did not seem like enough vindication. My mother got an alarm system installed in our house just in case he tried to retaliate.

The next day, I called the police and reported him. I do not know if the police ever pressed charges, but I was haunted by what the police officer said after taking my statement, "Do you have a boyfriend or a husband?"

"No, why?" I replied.

"Because things are not going to be the same again with your relationships. You might want to consider getting some help from a therapist."

What happened next is the reason why I am writing this book. I suffered through years of pain before being able to find my way back to a normal life. I don't want this to happen to you, and it doesn't have to. Healing can begin immediately. When I finally found what worked for me, the process of healing went quickly.

The next set of chapters is designed to help you process the pain and get a game plan for finding the love of your life. Although most of my experience has to do with sexual trauma, many of the lessons in this book also apply to abusive relationships. I will address both in the coming chapters.

Remember, this story has a good ending. I ended up marrying the man of my dreams.

Chapter 2: Common Reactions to Trauma

Whether you have experienced an abusive relationship or sexual trauma, most survivors will experience Post Traumatic Stress Disorder (PTSD) which changes the way you think and react to life's challenges. Below are common reactions to experiencing trauma that can impede your path toward finding love.

At first, you may not feel any emotions and you experience a general disassociation from your body. Next, you may have feelings of disbelief that you were actually attacked and a deep desire to forget it and move on. You may struggle with who is to blame for the attack or why it happened, or, in the worst case scenario, continues to happen. For example, a woman in an abusive relationship may think she is responsible for her partner's[1] rage. A

---

[1] Relationships and abuse can come in many combinations. For the sake of making my book easier to read I am assuming a female male relationship were the male is the attacker. I recognize that there are many men that would never commit these acts and acknowledge that men can also suffer tremendous pain in abuse relationships.

woman raped by a boyfriend may question her participation or compliance in the act.

Sex may seem transactional, or you may avoid it altogether. You may have a deep desire to find love but be totally frustrated, particularly when someone comes into your life and the relationship does not seem to get past the first three months or is only a superficial relationship.

Next, your mind starts forming strong opinions about yourself and your life. For example, you may doubt you will find someone or are capable of loving someone because of the attack.

You might settle into a high-alert method for dealing with potential threats. If you are in abusive relationship, you may become obsessed with your partner's feelings try to prevent the next outburst of rage. If you were raped, you may be fixated on preventing another attack. This fear controlling your life ironically feels safe and comfortable, but you know this is not a good way to live, let alone a good place to be when trying to develop a loving relationship.

You might also struggle with other relationships demanding trust or intimacy, like relationships with family, same-sex friends, or coworkers. In general, life seems hard, and your fear may expand to all aspects of your life. You let your guard down and you were attacked... well, no more bad things are going to happen on your watch! You have little tolerance for anyone who could compromise that, and avoid any type of conflict, or you go in the other direction and overreact with strong emotions. You may also feel extreme shame for the bad things that had happened to you and pull away emotionally from close friends and family to avoid discussions about the sexual trauma or what to do about your abusive partner.

The next few chapters discuss these roadblocks to love and offer words of advice on how to move through them and heal.

Chapter 3: Find a Therapist

Like a Sherpa who has knowledge and skillset to successfully navigate a climb of Mount Everest, a trained professional therapist can help you navigate your journey in healing.   Whether the attack happened recently or many years ago, if you are reading this book, then you need a therapist to get healthy. Time *does not* heal all wounds.

Be prepared to shop around for the right therapeutic style that meets your budget. In addition to asking your therapist about his or her credentials and degrees, ask the therapist to describe their process for helping patients. Therapeutic processes and orientations vary and it is important to get a therapist who is a good match for you. Some therapists will verbally participate in the sessions and give suggestions. Others take a passive role and ask you questions so that you can figure out your own solutions to life's challenges. If you don't know what therapeutic style would work best for you then go to two therapists and see what you prefer.

Lack of funds is not a reason to avoid getting help.   Group therapy sessions are usually lower priced than individual sessions. Churches, charities, and universities may also have therapists and support groups for a discount price or possibly free. Hotlines can help you in a time of crisis and can identify free services in your neighborhood for long term support. The following are examples of organizations that can help you:

Church support group
http://www.gatewaychurch.com/support-a-recovery/

Rape, Abuse, & Incest National Network (RAINN)
http://rainn.org/get-help

Safeplace http://www.safeplace.org/

Don't let fear prevent you from getting help. Some people believe going to a therapist may be a sign of weakness. You may be intimidated by facing your fears and admitting the event happened. You may tell yourself that if you don't go to therapy, then you don't have a problem. If you were attacked years ago and you never got help, find a therapist *now*. Don't let your fear of being labeled prevent you from getting help and becoming happy again. Telling yourself "I'm fine" is not good enough. Confronting your fear is a sign of strength and feeling good attracts good people into your life... like your husband!

It can be challenging to find a therapist who resonates and inspires you. The most important thing is to feel value from the sessions and start opening up. If you feel you are holding back or don't trust the therapist, try someone new. Don't go to a man if you don't feel comfortable talking to a man. Now is not the time to be fair. Now is the time to get help.

If you are depressed, you will tell yourself you should not go. Trust me, don't listen to a depressed mind. Don't even indulge it. Just go to a therapist. If the first one does not help, go to a second or third therapist. A bad therapist is not a reflection on you or your ability to heal yourself. Another therapist could be a better fit. Just keep trying and commit to searching for at least six months. Nothing is more important in your journey to love.

Once you have found a therapist you like, it is important not to judge or label yourself or discredit your ability to heal because one session did not work. Some sessions may be breakthroughs in your healing and others may not be that much value to you. That is normal.

I also recommend setting a goal with your therapist at the start of your therapy. You may find that the first therapist can help you get to a certain point in your treatment, and then another therapist will get you to the next stepping stone in your healing. It is ok to switch.

My therapist Jennifer liked to work in the present day. Instead of rehashing my childhood and what led up to my sexual abuse, we concentrated on everyday living and how past thoughts of abuse were affecting me today in my relationships. Then we replaced those thoughts with more rational, healthy thoughts. My relationships with other people dramatically improved. She is a licensed clinical social worker (LCSW). She asked questions but also had strong opinions. Sometimes, our sessions were Oprah "a-ha" moments, and other times I did not feel their value until a few days later. She was the sixth therapist I tried, based on a friend's recommendation. Our goal was to let go of my fear to find a loving, healthy relationship that would result in marriage.

The therapist I had right before Jennifer was crazy. A friend recommended him to me as well, and I had high hopes, because my friend had made so much progress in alleviating his psychological pain by working with this therapist. After a few sessions, the therapist told me that bad things were happening to me in this life because I had done bad things to people in a past life.

Not everyone working in the profession is sane. Just because a therapist says something about you in a session does not make that statement true. Move on if you get a bad vibe. I shudder to think what would have happened to me if I had given up after that bad experience and not contacted Jennifer.

Chapter 4: Heal Your Body

Immediately after you have been attacked, you may feel disconnect from your body, as if your soul is floating outside of your body watching from above. The first few days after my massage incident, I felt no physical pain whatsoever. I felt like I was in a movie, watching my life on screen. Everything seemed so surreal like I could hold my hand over a candle and feel no pain. This feeling of detachment from life is very common for someone suffering from Post Traumatic Stress Disorder (PTSD). I consider this time period God's version of painkillers after a major surgery. It gives you a short break before beginning life again. But don't be fooled into thinking you can stay in this phase for longer than a few days. You are meant to move forward with your life.

Next, I hated my body. I did not want to feel emotions, especially sadness. I no longer wished to be beautiful. I ate as much as I could. Again, eating to not feel attractive and considered "prey" to attackers is a protective mechanism that backfires on you in reaching your life goal of happiness. It also does not prevent attacks.

Healing begins with the body. I used to think working out and eating right was superficial but it prevents depression and improves your perspective on life. If you don't treat yourself well, you won't feel well. I recommend the following lifestyle changes that will aid your mental recovery from the trauma: exercise often, see your doctors, eat right, get enough sleep, and have fun.

Exercise Often

The most important thing to do after an attack, besides getting a therapist, is to exercise. If you have recently experienced a trauma, your body may be the last thing you want to connect to due to the pain but a healthy body is vital to feeling better emotionally. Go sign up for a self-defense class or take yoga. If you don't feel like being with others, then get an exercise video. Just be in your body and try to relax. Exercise is a great way to do that. Commit to thirty minutes three times a week with your doctor's approval.

Even if you don't feel like exercising, do it anyway. Depression often sucks the life out of you by taking away the pleasure out of common, everyday activity. Force yourself to exercise, and when your endorphins (chemicals in your brain) lift from the exercise, so will your depression. Be aware of any negative thoughts about exercise but don't indulge them--just go exercise. In fact, any time you feel awful, go exercise, even if it is just turning on music and dancing around your home for fifteen minutes. Here is what www.livestrong.com says about exercise and depression:

> "Exercise spurs the release of 'feel good' hormones in the brain -- such as neurotransmitters and endorphins -- which boost mood, helping to fight the common sad feeling experienced by depressive people. Exercise also affects brain neurotrophins, which help protect nerve cells from injury and transmit signals in the brain related to mood. Another mental benefit of exercise is it can increase self-confidence and promote goal-setting and positive thinking, helping depressed people feel more centered and hopeful about their lives." (Read more at http://www.livestrong.com/article/35679 1-exercise-to-overcome-depression/#ixzz2JQcuToho .)

The only caveat I have is to be safe and exercise in pairs during the day. If you exercise outdoors, always go with a friend. Don't put yourself at risk by jogging in a poorly lit park at midnight alone. I say this because you may be tempted to test your boundaries for another attack or deny the original attack happened.

See Your Medical Doctor

Schedule appointments with your doctors. If you have been sexually abused, your gynecologist can give you medical treatments for sexually transmitted diseases. Many sexually transmitted diseases have no symptoms and can block your fallopian tubes if untreated. Get a wide scan of tests to ensure you keep your fertility. As emotional as this step may be, it is crucial to your long-term health.

A general practitioner or internist can help design an overall health plan. You may have a medical condition that can make it more challenging to heal from your trauma. Besides giving advice on the best exercise and diet program for you, your doctor can also help identify anything that may make you susceptible to depression or anxiety. Are you low on iron, B-12, or vitamin D? You may need a vitamin shot or supplements. Do you have a thyroid disorder, hormonal imbalance, or sleep apnea? All these conditions can cause depression. I was diagnosed with sleep apnea and anemia.

Some doctors may prescribe prescription drugs for depression or sleep aids. If you are against taking sleep medication or pills for depression, find a doctor that has experience with natural or homeopathic cures.

I also recommend examining lifestyle changes with your doctor. Coffee, tea, and alcohol can cause anxiety and depression. Try quitting for a month, and see what happens to your sleep patterns and moods. In the first few days, you may experience withdrawal symptoms such as painful headaches. Your doctor can advise you how to get through this process.

Discuss all these options with your doctor and put a plan together for good health. I relied on talk therapy combined with lifestyle changes such as exercise, eating the right foods, and getting eight hours of sleep to cure the depression resulting from my attack.

Eat Right

My favorite foods to eat to improve my mood are salmon, spinach, eggs, walnuts, almonds, blueberries, kale, yogurt, and as many veggies that I can put in my mouth. Not only will this help you get healthy, it helps fight depression. Eating starchy sugary foods robs you from vitamins that stabilize your mood. Here is more helpful advice from the Livestrong Foundation:

> "Deficiencies in the B vitamins may lead to anxiety or depression. Consuming too much refined flour and sugar can deplete the B vitamins. A lack of vitamin B-12, or folic acid, has been linked to depression in clinical studies, according to Middle Tennessee State University. Eating fruit, green vegetables, dairy products, and fish, high in folic acid, can help improve moods. Deficiencies in selenium can contribute to anxiety, depression, and irritability. Foods high in selenium, including nuts, legumes, cereals, meat, dairy products, and fish, may normalize moods. Symptoms of omega-3 fatty acid deficiency include mood swings and depression, according to the University of Maryland Medical Center. Foods rich in omega-3s include cold-water fish such as

tuna, salmon, sardines, herring and mackerel, walnuts, soybeans and flaxseed in addition to walnut, flaxseed, canola and soybean oils." (Read more: http://www.livestrong.com/article/41372 2-depression-caused-by-diet/#ixzz2JQiCcTwk)

Also, depression is a medical condition in the brain, not just a feeling. Your ability to "feel happy" is linked to serotonin. Not surprisingly, eating nutritious foods, sleeping eight hours, and exercising all boost your serotonin levels. Below is more information on the link between serotonin and depression from www.livestrong.com:

> Serotonin is a brain chemical, or neurotransmitter, that sends messages within your brain and throughout your nervous system. Most serotonin, at least 75 percent, is located in the tissues of your gastrointestinal system and is involved in the movement of food through your intestines, but the remainder resides in your brain and is made primarily by neuronal cells of the pineal gland, according to the book *Human Biochemistry*. Within the brain, serotonin is involved in many processes such as regulating your mood, appetite, and sleeping cycle.

There are many neurotransmitters and hormones in your brain that contribute to how you feel and how you respond to certain situations, but serotonin is one of the most essential mood-regulating substances, according to the book *Human Physiology: An Integrated Approach*. High levels of serotonin are associated with happiness or contentment, whereas low levels are associated with anxiety, agitation, and depression. Serotonin synthesis is influenced by numerous factors, including emotional trauma, exposure to sunshine, eating certain food, and exercising.

Studies have shown that most forms of exercise increase the release of serotonin in your brain, according to the book *Exercise Physiology: Energy, Nutrition, and Human Performance*. Aerobic exercise increases serotonin levels in two ways: it directly increases the rate and frequency at which serotonin is released in your brain, and regular exercise increases tryptophan amino acid levels, which stimulate serotonin production secondarily.
(Read more:
http://www.livestrong.com/article/55437
0-bikram-yoga-
serotonin/#ixzz2JQjHbau5)

Yes, your thoughts also play a part in creating depression, but taking care of yourself physically is essential to preventing or healing from depression. Being sexually abused or physically attacked does not necessarily mean you will become depressed, but it can make you more susceptible to depression if you don't take good care of yourself. Don't create two problems for yourself. Prevent or heal as fast as you can from depression, and then get on with the recovery of abuse.

Get Enough Sleep

Do you get nightmares? If you have recently experienced sexual abuse or a major trauma you might have terror dreams of something chasing you, eating you or of falling out of the sky. Eventually you will dream that you are attacking your attacker and winning. I really got all my anger out in those dreams. Don't worry. You are not a killer. This is just your subconscious getting justice in your dreams. It is a sign that you are healing. If you have nightmares, tell yourself it is ok to fight back in your dreams right before you go to sleep. Remember your subconscious mind creates dreams and it loves suggestions!

Another issue in getting a good night's rest is fear. It may be very challenging for you to go to bed. I felt my most vulnerable at night, and often hid knives and baseball bats around the house to protect myself just in case I was attacked again. I recommend buying an alarm system, but if you can't afford that, pick up a cheap motion detector from Radio Shack. Also, do not live on the first floor of an apartment building or in a dangerous neighborhood. Consider moving or living with a friend for awhile. If you were attacked in your apartment, I highly recommend moving. If the managers at your apartment complex won't let you break the lease, then tell them you and ten of your closest friends will picket outside the leasing office. Tell the leasing office that you intend to hand out fliers to potential renters that a rape occurred in their complex, and that they won't let you out of the lease. Check with local law enforcement officials about permits and regulations. I guarantee the apartment management will let you out of the lease before you picket!

Put safeguards in place that make you feel secure, but also know that at some point, you have to let go of protecting yourself in order to have a good night's sleep. When you are able to overcome your fears and fully relax at night time, then you know you are healing. This is an important step in your recovery. Nowadays, I sleep like a log, no problems. It will happen to you, too.

Have Fun

Plan some fun activities for yourself. My favorite was taking a bath. The feel of the water on my skin helped me connect back with my body. You might also try meditation, watching a funny movie, or singing a happy song. When I was sad about a relationship with a boyfriend that did not work out, I used to sing the "Zip-a-Dee-Doo-Dah" song. I am convinced that it is impossible to cry when singing that silly song. Get your crazy song and sing out loud and proud when you feel sad.

After noticing the healthy changes in your body by following your overall health plan, the next step is to observe your thoughts. In the next chapter, we'll identify whether your thoughts are helpful or destructive in healing from the abuse.

Chapter 5: Heal Your Mind

The next phase of healing occurs in your mind. It has to do with what you are telling yourself about the trauma you endured, and what impact that has on the rest of your life. If you have read about PTSD, you have learned that after an attack your brain can function differently. When I first learned this, I took it the wrong way. I assumed I was "damaged goods." This is not a healthy approach to learning about what happened and how to get healthy. As much as you can, stop labeling or judging yourself.

YOGA
Shalabhasana
Locust pose

Also, start expecting positive change and healing. I remember when I first started yoga, and although I thought of myself as a flexible individual, the locust pose in Bikram yoga seemed particularly challenging. I could only lift my toes a few millimeters off the ground instead of a full extension. For months, I went to yoga class and tried this pose, with the intention of some day reaching the full extension. The day I reached the full extension, my yoga teacher praised me, and I felt pure joy. If you would have told me at the beginning that I would reach that pose in less than a year, I would have thought you were crazy, given the level of effort it took in the beginning. Your healing may follow the same path. Just as my yoga instructor did, I encourage you to concentrate more on your intention of where you want to go than where you are in any particular day. You will get there faster if your eyes are focused on the horizon, and acknowledge each day the work you performed to get there.

Although I used a physical example of healing above, mental healing can happen the same way and sometimes even faster than physical healing. Getting to the root of the disturbing thought does not take years of therapy. In the following sections, I will discuss how I healed by accepting what happened to me, understanding who to blame for the attack, and making peace with God and the universe.

Accept What Happened

First and foremost, you have to accept that what happened, actually happened.   This can be tremendously difficult for someone who was date-raped or abused by someone she loved. When the attack occurs in the normal parameters of a date or a dating relationship, it can sometimes be difficult to recognize it as abuse.   It might be construed as normal behavior. This is especially true if it happened when you first started dating, or if you have a limited frame of reference of what a healthy relationship actually looks like.

I remember sitting in my college dorm room, and we were all sharing details about the first time we had sex. My story was very different from the stories of the other girls, and I used words like, "He held my arms back when I resisted, but all in all it was not bad." I started to suspect something was wrong as I told my story, and the other girls had looks of shock and horror on their faces.   For the first time, I realized something was wrong.

The ability to even say the word "rape" or conceive that it could happen to me made me cry. It was much better to think that it was a sexual game or passionate lovemaking than accept the reality. But seeing these girls' faces made me realize I was just fooling myself. Don't get me wrong, I was a very smart girl, but I was dealing with a horrific act at a very young age, so I can understand why I chose denial as my coping skill. However, denial is not your friend. It prevents you from healing and forming an actual plan to protect yourself. You have to accept what happened before you can make different choices and live a better life.

I mentioned one form of denial in my earlier section about wanting to test your boundaries by putting yourself in dangerous situations, for example, running in a park alone at midnight. Another form of denial is to question the severity of what happened. You might have only been kissed strongly but in an inappropriate way. Maybe something much more involved occurred, or you might have experienced multiple, smaller events, but the cumulative effects make you doubt yourself. What matters is you are feeling emotional pain. If it is affecting your life, then go get help. Just accept that it happened first. Denial prevents you from making progress.

Another, more serious form of denial is continuing contact with your attacker or dating bad men. One reason why you may have a strong desire to remain friends or even continue to date your attacker is to avoid accepting what happened to you. You may also have a strong desire to be nice or be fair to your attacker or feel guilty that if you turned him in, he may have to suffer a severe punishment. You might tell yourself that if you let go of your feelings, don't rock the boat, and act in a certain, diplomatic way, you can rebuild a friendship as if "it" never happened. This gives you a false sense of control over the relationship.

In my midthirties, I was attracted to a guy who was not that great for me. After he pursued me for a year, I finally went on a date with him and we had sex. It was awkward and felt mechanical, mainly because we had not formed any basis for a loving relationship.   He did not call me for two months after that date. When he finally called at 6 pm on a Friday night and wanted to go out that same night, I turned him down. He explained that his work had sent him to Singapore for those two months, and that is why he did not call. I guess Singapore has crappy e-mail servers, too, but for the sake of being nice, I did not mention this flaw in his logic. He then told me he had gotten back with his old girlfriend who did not treat him well and wanted my advice. I felt obligated to meet him at the bar, since I had known him for so long, and I wanted to go back to our previous friendship.

We sat down at the bar and ordered drinks. His ex had moved back in with him, and he was telling me about this messed-up situation he had with her where he painted himself as the victim. He then switched his focus back to me and started flirting. Hint: any time a man's actions are incongruent with the words coming out of his mouth, run! I am serious. Make an excuse and get out of there! Telling you nothing is wrong and then doing something seriously offensive is the essence of why sexual abuse hurts so much. Your attacker is counting on your confusion about your feelings as a way to take advantage of you sexually.

I gave him a few words of advice about his girlfriend, said that I wanted to just be friends, and went home. I had mixed feelings about that night. A part of me enjoyed the fact that he was still sexually interested in me from our first encounter, but another part of me really just wanted to help him have a better relationship with his girlfriend.

When I told the story to my therapist Jennifer in our next session, I will never forget her reaction. She asked me, "Why do you want to be friends or even possibly date someone who has been so disrespectful to you?" I gave her three different answers, but she kept asking the question again, until finally I cried and realized why.

"If I am friends with him, then I control the situation. I can replace the hurt feelings with friendship. It makes the pain of being hurt go away. I am neutralizing his bad action with my good actions. It is because I don't want to accept that he hurt me or that I can get hurt again." It is then I realized how stupid that logic was, and that it was much healthier to just accept that he was an ass and move on. I had no obligation to be friends or continue contact. In fact, doing so prevented a healthy relationship with someone else from forming in my life. I did not make this mistake again.

Who to Blame?

The next big hurdle is who to blame. After accepting what happened, most women start to wonder why the event occurred and how to stop it from happening again. Inevitably, you may start with blaming yourself and pondering these questions: Did I say "No" loud enough? Did I want it to happen, but then feel guilty that it did? Did I not say "No" fast enough? Was it easier to just sit there and be out of my body while it was happening, than to accept the reality of what was happening? Did I deserve it by being too sexy? Was my flirtation and prior sexual actions giving permission? I was in a relationship with the man, so isn't that permission? We had already had sex, so isn't that permission? How can I feel love for someone who has treated me so badly? Am I insane?

Wanting to be desired by men, to be thought of as beautiful, or even wearing an inappropriate, sexy outfit is no invitation to a violent act of sexual abuse. It is normal to want to experiment with your sexuality, flirt, look sexy, and do sexual things. It is normal when touched to experience sensation in your body, regardless of whether you wanted the action to occur or not. It is also normal to not necessarily know how to handle every dating relationship or scenario at every age.

I remember messing around with this cute guy in my dorm room in college. He was smart, funny, and although we were not in a relationship, I enjoyed being around him. I wanted a good, sexual experience without drama, and this light encounter of kissing passionately had promise. When he started to lift my shirt, he stopped suddenly and asked if I were ok. He seemed generally concerned.

Verbally, I had given him no indication to stop. In fact, I was enjoying kissing him, but felt a little concerned about going to the next step. I was shocked that he could pick up on my slight discomfort so quickly. Then he said something I will never forget, "It is not fun for me if it is not fun for you. I don't want to do anything you don't want to do. How about we stop for tonight just to make sure?" When he left my dorm room, I started crying, knowing that was the way it was supposed to be. I finally got my answer to the question, "did I say no loud enough?" It does not matter how loud you say no, no is no.

Not all men will be emotionally tuned into your emotions, but they should be, especially if you are in a healthy, loving relationship. Forgive yourself fully of any actions or failure to act that you have associated with the attack you suffered. In fact, recognize that blame really does not help. Does it really matter if you get the correct percentage blame assigned to each contributing factor? Does making yourself feel shameful help in healing? No. Shaming never works and can often leads to bad coping skills. You did not do anything wrong. A healthier approach is to put together a new plan for dating, which I will explain in chapter 9: "Lower Your Guard Without Being Vulnerable in Dating."

Before I continue, I want to warn you about opening up to people who are not therapists. Although, sometimes this can be rewarding and healing, some people may react differently or even weirdly inappropriately when finding out what happened to you. You should realize that sexual abuse is common. During her talk show[2] with guest star Tyler Perry, Oprah estimated that one in four women and one in six men experience sexual trauma. That statistic amounts to a lot of people in many different stages of recovery, or even perhaps denial. These people might encourage you to just get over it or even avoid you because they don't want to deal with what happened to them or a loved one. When you are raw and in pain, you expect people to help you, and when the opposite happens, it can throw you for a loop.

My advice is to join a group therapy session if you feel the need to connect with others about the attack. I also would choose wisely who you tell in your circle of friends and family. Start slowly when describing what happened, and if you don't get a positive reaction, don't worry about what that

---

[2] The show originally aired on November 25, 2010. For more information please visit: http://www.oprah.com/showinfo/A-Two-Day-Oprah-Show-Event-200-Men-Who-Were-Molested-Come-Forward_1

means. Remember, some people may just not know what to say or feel horrible that they cannot take your pain away immediately. This is especially true for parents of a teenage daughter who is date-raped. They may feel a moral obligation to protect you and feel as if they failed miserably. You might also feel tempted to blame them. I encourage you to reframe your thinking: your parents are victims, too. Few people naturally have all the skill sets to properly react to a sexual assault, and this includes your parents. As you start to forgive yourself for what you may or may not have done, then I encourage you to also forgive those around you, like your parents, and realize the horrific act was caused by one person...your attacker.

There are a few things you should know about people who commit sexual abuse. They have a game plan to seduce and confuse you to get what they want. It is their goal to keep it a secret, because if you tell other people, you will easily decode their faulty logic. Just as the massage therapist tried to comfort me with, "it's just part of the massage," they will say things and act in ways that are incongruent with the actual, violent act they are committing. Your mind is already raw from the attack, and they would like to convince you that you participated in it, and, therefore, you agreed and are guilty, too. Don't believe it.

In the case of date rape or relationship rape, your attacker may just be begging you to do something you don't want to do so that he can feel pleasure. Your desire to please your loved one can result in tremendous internal conflict with your own morals, sexual desires, and knowledge of what is right for you. Someone who cares for you would never ask you to do something you don't want to do.

You might also be tempted to contact your attacker and confront him face-to-face. My recommendation is to spend at least one year in therapy before trying this. In my heart, I believe you will get more satisfaction yelling at a pillow representing your attacker on your therapist's couch or writing a letter to your attacker that you never send. Beside the danger of being around a bad person, you might also not get the satisfaction of closure you deserve. The attacker may have a totally different opinion of what happened and degrade you for having extreme emotions. He might also try to form a relationship with you again that would be unhealthy. The best thing for you to do is to stay away from your attacker, even if it was your parent or a boyfriend or husband you really loved, and it happened only that one time.

Although I have never experienced incest or childhood sexual abuse, my heart goes out to you if you have. I believe that it must be similar to rape, but with some of the themes amplified—lack of control, hopelessness, extreme guilt that you cannot protect your body, the betrayal of trust, and a desperate need to please a loved one or authority figure. Because I have been attacked multiple times over a period of years, I understand that the first time it feels as if the life is being crushed out of you, like an antelope caught in the mouth of a lion. You feel hopeless. After the second or third attack, you learn to disassociate from your body. You actually leave your body and float on the ceiling for a while. Whatever you did to survive, it is ok. Even if you faked a relationship, made nice to pretend it did not happen, or felt love for someone who was supposed to love you but did not, it's ok. Even if you participated in the sexual act, liked it, or explored your sexuality within it, it's ok. If bad things continue to happen over a period of time, your mind will do crazy things to survive or avoid the horror of the truth. Whatever you did to stay whole and try to make things feel normal, love and accept yourself as a brave soul.

It may also be incredibly hard for you with respect to blame. Make no mistake about it; the person who attacks a child is the most disgusting piece of shit who walks the face of the planet. Just because you were the target does not make you part of that shit. Just because you share DNA does not make you dirty. These assholes are so hated that criminals in prison execute them. Think about that for a minute. Criminals have no problem killing them. Someone who has committed serious crimes and is serving time has no problem thinking that a child molester is beneath him and not worthy of life.

It is one of the hardest things to deal with if you loved your attacker. It is ok to have mixed feelings in this situation, too. The desire to have loving parents, relatives, or husband is very strong and so natural. From an evolutionary standpoint, humans have been living in small groups for safety for thousands of years. But don't let your desires for these specific relationships prevent you from accepting what has happened and placing blame on the attacker. If you have to lose a parent or possibly someone you have dated for years to get healthy, it is worth it. Remember, you can also replace these unhealthy relationships in your life with healthy alternatives. You can find other human beings who will satisfy these fundamental needs in healthy ways.

Making Peace with God and the Universe

It is a very common reaction to blame God and distrust the universe. When I forgave myself and finally blamed my attackers, there was an uneasy feeling about what this meant with my relationship to God, and how I felt about the universe. Why did God let this happen to me, let alone multiple times by multiple individuals? How can I continue to live in a world that has such horrifying acts of violence? (FYI, these are very common feelings of anyone suffering from PTSD.)

Although everyone's search for the answer to these questions will be different, I believe strongly that we are all given a choice... free will. Sometimes, people choose badly and hurt others. It is just that simple. I do not believe that God intended you to be abused. God put you on this planet to do great things. No matter how bad it was, what happened to you, I strongly believe that God, the universe, and you can turn that into something good in terms of personal growth and emotional development, if you are open to it. It takes awhile to get there, but remember God uses shit to make beautiful roses in the garden. Not that anyone deserves pain or needs pain to get to the next level spiritually, but think of it more as God using your deepest pain to help your soul rise to new heights. You thought you could crush her? Well, look at her soar!

Another way to make peace with God is to give the problem back to God to solve. In the book *The Shack*, the author says that in order to accept God after an attack, you must accept that God will also follow-up on Her promise for justice. God made the attacker, and God will deal with the choices the attacker made when the attacker dies. It is God's mess to clean up. God will also heal those who felt the pain of the attack.

Letting go of your need to "make right" the attack is healthy. If it helps you to believe that God will solve it later, then I encourage you to do so. If you choose to report it to the police or authorities, then do that. If you want to beat up a pillow that represents your attacker on a therapist's couch, then do that. Whatever it is you need to do to feel justice has been served, do it and then let it go. It is more important for you to take action and let it go than what ultimately happens to the attacker.

Part of accepting what happened to you is also accepting that bad things can happen to you in all aspects of your life. As Albert Einstein said, "I think the most important question facing humanity is, 'Is the universe a friendly place?' This is the first and most basic question all people must answer for themselves." Einstein was referring to countries developing technology. If they feared the universe, they would focus their efforts on protection, that may, in turn, cause their own destruction. The quote continues, "For if we decide that the universe is an unfriendly place, then we will use our technology, our scientific discoveries, and our natural resources to achieve safety and power by creating bigger walls to keep out the unfriendliness and bigger weapons to destroy all that which is unfriendly, and I believe that we are getting to a place where technology is powerful enough that we may either completely isolate or destroy ourselves as well in this process."[3]

Who knew Einstein was an expert on hyper-vigilance and PTSD! Who knew countries could suffer the same fate? This quote may help you see that protecting yourself at all costs in the face of fear is a coping mechanism known to all of humanity, but this skill does not give you a happy and prosperous life. In the 1980s classic movie *War Games*, Matthew Broderick accidently starts a computer simulation of global nuclear war with the US government defense

[3] This quote was found on this website:
http://www.awakin.org/read/view.php?tid=797

systems, which results in the computer activating its nuclear weapons against Russia in real life. Matthew has to teach the computer to lower its weapons to save the world, but regardless of how Matthew interacted with the computer in the simulation, the end result was total world annihilation. Finally, he has the computer play itself in the game to realize that no player wins with such acts of aggression and fear. I can still hear the computer saying, "Shall we play a game?"

It can be very unsettling at first to think that you could be attacked again or that even something worse could happen. I struggled to accept this realization with my therapist Jennifer for many months. I resisted learning skills for coping, because it was a way of reminding myself it could happen again. My focus was preventing an attack, not how to fight back. Again, this is a very unhealthy way of looking at treatment. The enormous amount of energy it takes to stay vigilant to an attack will zap you of your peace. If you are always on guard for an attack you will destroy your sense of peace and happiness. I finally realized that bad things could happen *to me*, but that does not mean that the end result has to be bad *for me*. I *can* survive, over and over again. I can learn more and more about myself and what I can do next time to make it easier to deal with pain and perhaps create a new outcome altogether. Since I accepted this statement fully, I have not suffered another sexual attack. When you regain your sense of self and self-esteem, you are not afraid to be truly present in your life, feel all the emotions of the moment, and take healthy actions that create new outcomes.

You cannot control another person's actions, thoughts, or feelings, but you can control your own. Do not discount the enormous power of being present in your body, in control of your thoughts, and having a well-thought-out game plan that cannot only reduce the likelihood of an attack occurring in the first place, but also get you back to a normal, healthy life as quickly as possible.

My life is truly powerful, and I feel at peace with God and the universe. I know God will bless me for writing this book. When I receive a phone call from someone who struggled so long to find peace after being attacked and achieved it after reading this book, my soul will soar. This is God turning my shit into roses.

Chapter 6: Avoid Common Dating Mistakes

After a period of time, you will want to rejoin the human race and begin dating again. If you have followed this book and worked closely with your therapist, you may avoid some of the common pitfalls that I am about to describe.

The Madonna or Slut Coping Mechanism

Most people who have been abused either avoid sex altogether or sleep with everyone they can. The objective of both strategies is the same: to be in control and avoid getting hurt. Again, these coping mechanisms occur when you are in denial about the attack, blaming yourself, or not taking full responsibility for getting help. They are ineffective crutches that cripple your ability to find healthy, long-lasting love.

I was someone who avoided sex and intimacy. When I was in high school and my early college years, I loved dating guys who did not want sex or went extremely slow. I had several boyfriends who had experienced their own trauma but not necessarily sexual abuse. These relationships were very healing for me, as I learned to trust men again, but none of them evolved into more than friendships with light kissing.

In my twenties, I changed my focus to my career. When other women were starting families, I proudly announced that I would not get married before thirty. I wanted to see the world, and I did. I took grueling jobs, easily working eighty-hour weeks, flying internationally, leaving me no time for a social life or forming a love connection.   I ran my body ragged and became susceptible to depression, trying to make sense of the tragedy that had happened to me.

It is not wrong to pursue your career or find joy from achievement unless you are purposely doing it to avoid love. Don't get me wrong. I wanted a deep, meaningful relationship, but I was scared about what to do with it if I ever found it. Since some of my attacks occurred when I was in dating relationships, the thought of intimacy really scared me, as I felt I would be opening myself up for another attack. I never shared my deepest thoughts with the men I dated.   My relationships were superficial or intellectual but never emotional. I did have good guy friends whom I had feelings for, but I always kept them at a distance sexually. I was also attracted to men who had issues with intimacy, who I knew would not commit.

Here is the funny thing about attraction. You can believe so strongly that you are attracted to a particular person when you are actually just in need of something. When you satisfy the need, the unhealthy attraction goes away immediately.

Here is a trick to end an unhealthy attraction. If you are having trouble letting go of someone who you know is bad for you, write on a sheet of paper three emotions that you feel most strongly when you are in his presence. For example, you feel sexy, confident, peaceful, in control, passionate... you get the point. Make sure to actually write them down on the paper before you read the next sentence.

What you wrote down is what you desire for yourself and what is keeping you from leaving him. If you knew you could feel this way without him, you would leave immediately. It is your need and deep fear that you can't feel that way alone that keeps you attracted.

Now, for each characteristic, write down three ways you can give that gift to yourself and create that feeling without him. When you self-fulfill your needs, you attract healthy life partners who amplify those feelings in a healthy way. You have a sense of enjoyment, sharing your life with your partner who has a common value system. This is very different from the destructive need to control the relationship because you are hungry, desperate, and willing to sacrifice your own moral high ground by dating someone who is not right for you in order to get your needs met.

Another way people cope with sexual abuse is to become sexually promiscuous. Sex becomes transactional, and you have the false sense you are in control. In a similar way to the woman who is jogging the poorly lit park at midnight, your desire is to test your boundaries to prove to yourself that bad things won't happen again or maybe never even happened in the first place. Being sexual within hours of knowing someone is a Russian roulette game that somehow gives you a sense of control. If he does not like you, "who cares, because the chances of it working out are so slim anyway." You want to explore your sexuality and feel a high, intense emotion. Not knowing how it will end provides heightened drama. The act of sex itself gives you a false sense of intimacy that you crave. You might also devalue your body and discount your deepest desire to be loved and respected. You might also generalize that all men are self-absorbed, thoughtless and avoid commitment. You want sex, so why not just avoid the messy, emotional part of the relationship where you can get seriously hurt.

If you were raped by a boyfriend who you loved, the fear of being betrayed like that again feels unbearable and will prevent you from making healthy choices in your life. You may become a Madonna or slut or both at different times in your life if you don't get help and resolve your issues of self-esteem and self-worth.

In the case of the Madonna coping mechanism, you doubt your ability to have a healthy relationship, so you avoid sex altogether. The fear of being raped by a stranger or being in a situation out of your control makes you hyper-vigilant to threats, leaving you little room to develop trust or love with someone.

If you choose promiscuity, then you are ruining every relationship before it starts. Having sex before you know someone well puts the relationship on full-speed from the start and does not allow for softer, less dramatic moments in which to get to know someone. You may overreact to his actions, and often the man pulls away after the mystery of sleeping with you is gone. He may even refer to you as crazy or "a lot of baggage". All of these interactions tear down your self-esteem and strengthen your belief that men are no good.

Regardless of what coping mechanism you might choose, you will notice that both styles are categorized by high-drama moments. The Madonna avoids the moment. The promiscuous woman can't get enough intensity. Both have confused sex with intimacy and love. Sex is now the focal point of their thoughts and the highest motivator in their actions in their relationships with men.   Sex is the bartering tool for affection or control.   Sex is often used in a destructive pattern that results in loss of self-esteem, disconnection with the body, and lost hope that love is possible.   This is not how normal, healthy relationships work.

Before I describe how to form a healthy, loving relationship with someone special, I need to get inside your head and eliminate your negative thoughts. Please don't skip this next chapter, as it is the foundation to finding true love.

Chapter 7: Debunk Negative Thoughts

Most people who are sexually abused experience PTSD. You become hyper-vigilant, have intrusive thoughts or flashbacks, may overreact to everyday threats, or tend to see the world differently than those who have not had the same experiences you have had. You can also become situationally depressed with feelings of hopelessness, low self-worth, or even suicide.

When it comes to dealing with negative thoughts, I always remember this *Mad TV* skit in which Bob Newhart is a therapist. Mo Collins walks into Bob Newhart's office and starts talking about her problems, and then looks up at Bob the therapist and says, "What should I do?"[4]

The therapist shouts loudly, "Stop it!" She looks puzzled. The therapist speaks again, "It's all in your head. Stop it!"

"Sorry?" she replied.

---

[4] This is not a word for word quotation of the skit. I summarized for the sake of brevity. The video can be found on YouTube at http://www.youtube.com/watch?v=LhQGzeiYS_Q.

"I said stop thinking those thoughts! S-t-o-p i-t!" the therapist explains.

She starts explaining another problem, and the therapist interrupts again, "Stop it! That sounds awful. No wonder you feel so sad. You don't want to go through life thinking that thought, do you, so just stop it!"

Getting rid of negative thoughts in your head is very similar to this skit. The first and foremost part of the process is to realize that not all your thoughts are true or helpful. A depressed mind lies to you. It likes to take the half-truth about what you observe in life and spin it into a broad generalization that causes pain.

Change Your Mind, Change the Outcome

Realizing that the way I saw the world had been compromised after the attacks I experienced and that the thoughts I had in my head were not real made me feel incredibly uncomfortable at first. I felt so strongly these thoughts were "my truth." My therapist Jennifer reminded me again and again to be open to a different, more practical manner of solving life's challenges, and then the outcome you think is so certain will change. Like is a self-fulfilling prophecy: when we indulge negative thoughts, we also look for the negative outcome as proof that our thoughts are real. But as we change our perspective, so does the outcome change, and eventually our intense feelings lessen.

Once you learn a process for defeating those negative thoughts, your confidence will return, and you will start changing your life. You will start feeling more comfortable in your own skin. People will react to you differently. Even people you hate, who you thought would never change, will treat you differently.

Just as you can look at a dog and immediately know its intentions (attack dog or friendly, play dog), when you feel extreme emotions, other people react to you strongly, too. The worse you feel inside, the more people react to you in negative ways. People pick up on your body language and act accordingly.

When you are hyper-vigilant, you often try to make everyone feel good or control the outcome so that bad things don't happen. When bad things do happen, you inappropriately blame yourself for not preventing the event. What you think influences your body language, tone of voice, and energy level.

Other people may subconsciously pick up on your guilty feelings by reading your body language and start to blame you, too. Manipulative people will use your guilt against you and take advantage of this.

My husband Aaron helped me realize this principle at work. Often, I was so hung up on making everything perfect and taking responsibility for other people's feelings that I accepted blame inappropriately. For example, I planned a social activity for a few of my coworkers to mingle at our corporate suite during a concert at the Toyota Center in Houston. One of my coworkers was bringing his wife as a birthday surprise. My administrator had given me six, full-access tickets and one, limited-access ticket that was only for the corporate suite and required the user to buy an entrance ticket to the concert. As luck would have it, I gave the limited-access ticket to my coworker, who, in turn, gave it to his wife. When my coworker got to the stadium and could not use the ticket, he was angry and called me multiple times. My husband reminded me that the bad ticket was not my fault. My administrator had not told me about the ticket's limitation, and I had not purposely tried to ruin my coworker's plans. I also had offered to either trade tickets or buy my coworker a concert ticket for his wife. He was so upset, however, that he and his wife went home and missed the concert.

After the concert, my husband warned me that my coworker may try to blame me again. He said it was very important to not accept blame, and, instead, act surprised at his intense reaction. "After all, you offered him two easy solutions to the problem, but he wanted to stay angry."

The next day at work, just as my husband predicted, my coworker approached me, wanting to blame me for the event. Although I doubted my husband's advice and worried this approach would make my coworker more angry, I did not accept blame or say, "I'm so sorry." I calmly explained my administrator had made a mistake. The ticket limitation was printed on the card itself, and just like me, he could have also read the message before the event. I also had offered him two solutions to the problem at the time. I was amazed at my coworker's reaction. He backed down quickly. He saw how calm I was and questioned his own reasoning. He then admitted he overreacted and apologized.

When you become more self-aware of self-defeating thoughts and separate your identity from a negative event or person, others will appear less intense or maybe not blame you at all. When they see your body language as calm, they will start to question if their own assumption about your guilt is indeed correct.

In other words, if you are always feeling crappy, guilty, or awful about yourself, you will hold your body in a weak position, speak in certain tones, be overly defensive, and display other bad habits that reinforce these same negative thoughts in other people's minds. When you learn to defeat these thoughts, you are less susceptible to attack or intense emotion. Just as a sick animal represents easy prey, a depressed mind can encourage others to attack and blame you if something goes wrong. A healthy animal (calm, rational, assertive person) is a challenge to defeat. A predator may get injured in the attack (be wrong about my assumption) and will search for easier prey (look for a different explanation of events).

The Process for Eliminating Negative Thoughts

The best place to fight negative thoughts is on paper. When you are analyzing events in your head, it can be tough to identify the faulty logic. My favorite way to debug my negative thoughts is delineated below:

Step 1: Write down your negative thoughts. What am I afraid will happen, or what do I believe about myself that makes me feel sad or hopeless? Get it all out as if you are throwing up. It keeps coming up. Shoot for at least ten crappy thoughts swimming around in your head. They do not have to be about the sexual attack or abusive boyfriend you suffered, either. They can be about your ability to be successful at work or finding the love of your life. For example, "I messed up that report, and my boss is going to know I am incompetent at this job. I am useless at my job." Another example is, "The last three dates I had with Joe did not go well, and I think he is no longer interested in me. I can't keep someone's attention for longer than a month, and I am too old to find love. I missed my window of time to get married." Example three, "My dad never loved me. I keep overcompensating on dates, or I lose interest quickly. I can't relax. I can't find someone who I really love or have intense feelings for."

It can seem incredibly scary to face your fear when you do this the first time, but when you see the results of this exercise, you won't be able to wait to do it again. The only trick is not to write your emotions like this, "I feel sad." You need to get to the thought and the event that is creating that emotion.

Step 2: Write down the event or its trigger. Go back through your thoughts, and try to identify something that happened near-term that has caused this thought to enter your conscious mind. For example, you could have watched a movie in which someone is beat up or raped, and your negative thought is that you cannot protect yourself from future attacks. In my previous examples from step 1, the messed-up report and Joe's perceived indifference on a date are the events or triggers.

Notice that example three in step 1 does not have an event or trigger. Although you may be tempted to say the event is that my dad never loved me, you should be looking for something that happened to you within two weeks that is reinforcing this thought pattern, for example, rejection for a date, or someone not calling you back when he said he would. Something that happened that is similar to how your dad mistreated you and that makes you feel that love is impossible.

Before I continue to step 3, I want to talk a little more about triggers and PTSD. Your mind is constantly changing. I mean, the physical structure of your brain is changing. As you think thoughts and feel emotions, your brain stores these patterns physically by creating neural pathways. The more thoughts you have that are similar, the more electrical impulses fire that reinforce this pattern and structure. A trigger is an event, something someone says, or moment that occurs in everyday life that reminds you of your past attack. When you witness a trigger, your brain maps that back to a neural pathway, and you start to experience feelings and emotions from previous, similar events that happened to you in your life. That is why, before you were raped, a movie that has violence may not be so upsetting to watch, but watching the same movie after you were raped may cause you to cry uncontrollably in pain. You are actually reliving the trauma, because your brain is connecting the movie to your past attack.

This is also why I say don't indulge a depressed brain. When a brain is depressed, it hungers for reinforcement that the universe is unsafe. The trigger is the half-truth, and your negative thought is the generalization. An event that you witness in your life that is in reality a two out of ten in terms of intensity is now suddenly registering as an eight, because your brain is mapping it back to a tragic event or depressed thought.

A turning point in my healing occurred when I began not to trust my brain. Instead of feeling something, I questioned it; talked back to it. I built new neural pathways that were healthy. Have you heard of muscle memory, when your body adapts to exercise that you do repeatedly? Think of this process as building emotion memory. The more you write down on a piece a paper your fears and depressed thoughts and debunk them, the more your brain learns this response to a depressed thought. Now, I can debunk a depressed thought in my mind the moment it pops up. This is the peace you crave. You are decoupling events and triggers from your overall sense of self and self-worth. The thought is a thought; it is not you. You are not mapping back everyday thoughts and feelings to the intense emotions of the attack. Life is easier because you are no longer overreacting and you can come up with practical solutions. Life does not feel like World War III because the trigger is disconnected from the bomb of this awful thought or event.

Step 3: Debug the negative thought. Now it is time to talk back to the thought and change your neural pathways to build a healthier brain. For each thought, consider the following questions below, and see if you can identify the faulty reasoning behind your depressed thought.

- **Is it true?** Before you say yes, reexamine it closely again. In every situation, every time, with every interaction, will the result be the same again? Is there any scenario you can imagine where the result would be different, or this statement would be invalid? I would find it hard to believe if your answer to this question "Is it true?" is always yes, since rarely in life does anything fit nicely into black and white buckets. The universe has endless possibilities, both good and bad--it is damn hard to come up with a statement that is universally awful and has a negative outcome occurring 100 percent of the time. Anyway, it is important to answer the question for each negative thought and to come up with examples that are not true, as this process mentally restructures your mind and breaks down those negative, neural pathways.

- **Does believing this statement help me accomplish my goals?** Even if this is true, which hopefully I have proven that it is not, does believing this statement enrich your life or make you happy? Again, this relates back to Bob Newhart's "stop it" comment. If believing a negative thought is not helping you reach your goals, than why believe it?

What benefit is it to mentally punish yourself? Ok, I know what you are going to say: "To be prepared for the worst." If you think this statement is true, you are most likely hyper-vigilant and not considering rational solutions to problems. Be open to a different way of dealing with problems versus just fearing what will happen to you

- **Is it realistic?** Life is meant to have ups and downs. You are meant to be challenged by certain circumstances and not always feel great about outcomes. Think about the reverse. If everything came your way easily, would you give up trying? Do you learn more from your failures than your successes? Look at life as an adventure with the expectation that sometimes you are supposed to fail, but that does not doom you to a horrible life. For example, maybe you did fail at the work report, but did you really expect to work your entire life without messing up once? Does your boss expect you to be perfect 100 percent of the time? If you answer yes, I dare you to ask her that question. Most likely, your boss expects you to grow and learn from your mistakes versus being perfect. If your boss answers yes, than you are in an unstable work environment and you should get out. As for dating, did you really expect to meet the man of your dreams on the first date? If you did, would you trust it? Having bad experiences strengthens your ability to define your values, wants, and needs. It provides clarity to your decisions, because you know what you don't want.

- **Do I need more data before I can accurately draw this conclusion?** Think like a scientist testing a hypothesis. Do you have a natural bias toward concluding a certain meaning from a limited set of data? Could there be multiple factors causing the event to occur, and not just a deficiency on your part? For example, you turned in the bad report at work, and your boss did not look pleased. What else is influencing your boss's reaction? Could the company not be doing well financially? Could your boss have been criticized by someone else and be in a bad mood? As for the dating example, what else is going on in Joe's life? Did an ex-girlfriend call him, and is he considering getting back together with her? Is he questioning his own sexuality? Is he dating you to fulfill his mother's expectation of what a good girlfriend is? I recommend coming up with at least four other possibilities for what the trigger means, besides relating it back to the depressed thought.

- **What other outcomes could occur?** Our brains like simple solutions and enjoy patterns, but the universe has endless possibilities. We often like to jump to a negative conclusion versus dealing with not knowing what will happen. For example, do you know for certain how your boss will react to your report? Maybe the report is not your best work, but maybe your boss does not care and just needed to get something done. Remember, most times the worst thing does not happen. Most times, something new happens that you can't predict. As for the dating scenario, maybe Joe dumps you. Maybe you decide it is actually you who was bored on the date and decide to dump him. Maybe he goes back to his ex and then runs back to you, ready for a full commitment. Maybe tomorrow you wake up and you meet the man who is really destined to be your husband and Joe becomes a faded memory. The important thing is to stay open to the possibility of change and trust your ability to make good decisions in reaction to events outside your control. For each negative thought, list four alternate opportunities and different ways you could respond if the negative event did occur.

- **Besides giving up, what else can I do to influence this situation in a calm and assertive manner?** A depressed mind loves to feel hopeless, as if nothing you can do will break the thought pattern. It can even drain your energy, making you feel worthless and paralyzed. When you write down your thoughts on paper, however, and use the rational "thinking" part of your brain to come up with solutions to problems, your energy level changes. Options create power and different outcomes. When you go numb and just feel pain, you surrender this useful tool. Stay in your body and come up with new ideas. In the work example, you could acknowledge that maybe it was not your best work, but your boss is a rational person and will base his opinion of you on multiple events and interactions. You can release your fear and concentrate your energy on the next assignment. You could also seek feedback on how to improve from either a colleague or mentor at work. You could possibly even take a class, either from your company or an outside industry workshop that would improve your writing ability or knowledge on the subject, so your next report is better. As for the dating situation, you could choose to date other people besides Joe. You could choose to detach from Joe and put your energy into other efforts, such as friends or work. You could choose to just stay open to the possibility of love, whether that is Joe or someone else, recognizing you don't have to control the relationship for love to happen.

- **What advice would I give a good friend if she told me this?** When we see our problems from a third-person perspective, we often gain clarity on their solutions. Pick up a pillow, imagining the pillow is you, and you are your best friend. What advice would you give to the pillow? Another tactic is to write a letter to yourself, but as if you were writing from the perspective of a third person, like a close friend, favorite author, God, or maybe even Oprah. Pick someone who you admire and who would act only in loving kindness toward you. What would that person tell you to do right now to improve your life and feel better?

- **How long should I suffer this fate?** Ok, what if you did do something totally awful? How long should you be punished for this act? A month, a year, ten years? What if this was a court of law? What would a jury say? Would a group of human beings agree with you that you are unlovable, unable to work, or completely worthless? Or would they feel compassion for you, given your circumstances, and identify with you, as this is the human experience. Suffering endlessly is torture, not motivation. Accept what you did or failed to do, and then let go of your guilt. Then talk back to your negative thought, and recognize that you are not condemned to worry and pain for the rest of your life because you made a mistake.

- **Is this helpful criticism that I am overreacting to?** Often, we are influenced by a negative authority figure such as a boss, parent, or bad teacher when we create a negative generalization of ourselves. We map helpful criticism back to the mean things these people told us and feel overpowered or that an injustice has occurred. Look at the criticism for what it is. How bad would it be if it were true or a piece of it were true? Am I stuck and unable to grow? If I recognized the criticism as justified, could I change my behaviors instead of shaming myself? Is it even the same critical thing my dad, teacher, or other authority figure said? Maybe I am overreacting because it sounds similar, whereas, if I kept a cool head, I could even learn from it. If I make positive change as a result of the criticism, then I defeat the belief I am no good, that I can't change or improve my circumstances, and disprove the authority figure's negative opinion of me-- triple healing for the price of one. Your self-esteem will soar.

- **Is this based on one person's opinion?** At times, we can overemphasize either a comment or one person's power in our life. If you feel threatened by what one person said, start asking if this person's belief system is the same as yours. If not, why is it more valuable than yours? Do other people agree with this person's assessment of you? Can you come up with a list of people who would disagree with what this person is saying? Are you destined to go through life with this negative person in control of your future, or can you distance yourself from this person and his or her opinion of you?

- **Am I being a perfectionist?** Do you have outrageous expectations of yourself? Are you saying things have to be absolutely perfect for you to feel happy? Think about small children learning to walk. If they don't get up the first time, do you think they are of no value? As adults, we sometimes have outrageous expectations of ourselves when we are trying to learn new skills, or, in our cases, healing from sexual attacks or abusive relationships. If things don't happen perfectly, we deem our efforts as failures. How can you behave more compassionately and more loving toward yourself, as you learn and grow from your mistakes? What expectation or standard do you need to let go of that is actually preventing you from growth or experiencing new things in life?

- **Am I ignoring the good?** Are you overexaggerating one negative aspect and crowding out the benefit of everything else? Are you discounting any of your achievements? Every time we complete the standing portion of Bikram yoga, the instructor asks us to acknowledge our efforts in the mirror. Recognize the value in trying and the courage it takes to change.

I realized that, intellectually, I could not succeed if I had such horrible thoughts about myself, my ability to affect the world around me, or my ability to cope with life's challenges. I do this exercise even today to get rid of the "noise," reduce anxiety, or just prepare for a difficult challenge. As you repeat this activity, you will notice your thought process naturally change to more healthy ones.   See the table below to identify any of these negative thoughts that you must learn to talk back to, and to find out where you are in your stage of healing.

(Note to readers: I originally planned to organize this information below as a table but unfortunately tables with three or more columns are very hard to format in books with small dimensions. Therefore I have organized this table in paragraph form. Column one is the negative thought, column two is the trigger, and column three is the rational response.)

Table 1: Negative thoughts, triggers, and rational responses

Negative thought: What if I never find love?

Trigger: The guy I have been dating for two months just broke it off with me. I wasn't that attracted to him, either.

Response: Ok, this guy did not work out, nor the last (fill in your number). So what? It only takes one to get married, and in the grand scheme of things, I have not dated that many people compared to the six billion people on earth. I can recognize that I am just feeling uncomfortable not knowing what my future holds, but this thought does not help me reach my goals. In reality, I am lucky this guy broke up with me and did not waste anymore of my time. Many of my friends are married, which means that I can get married, too. Maybe I should have dumped him sooner? Can I also accept the fact that I don't know the actual date when I will meet my husband? Can I accept the fact that I might never get married? Feel the pain, but notice how this fear may be controlling you. When you are looking for love, the last thing you want is fear dictating your reactions. Dedicate your life to finding your future husband and be open to love, but also love yourself now and create a fun life for yourself right now. Your husband should accentuate your good life, not be the sole basis for it.

Negative thought: What if I am incapable of love?

Trigger: I went on three dates with a nice guy, yet I do not feel those loving feelings. I am not sure I am attracted to him.

Response: Unless you have received a very bad blow to your frontal lobes (the front part of your brain that controls personality and emotional functioning), your ability to feel love should be intact. Recognize it takes time, both to heal from the past and build trust. Maybe, start with a smaller goal of developing friendships with good, quality men. Also, pay attention and honor your feelings about attraction. If you are not ready to do something sexual, that is ok. And if you are not sexually attracted to a good guy, that is ok, too. Sometimes God places good men in your life to get you ready for your husband. It is ok to "practice" with safe dating that is not intense.

Negative thought: What if his interest in me ends right after I sleep with him?

Trigger: The guy I am dating is sexually intense. I can tell he wants to go to the next level. I really like him, but sometimes he is flighty and doesn't call me until the last minute.

Response: Trust your gut. If you don't feel trust, then he is not the right one for you. Dating games can provide you with intensity and drama, but in the end do not build trust. If you are deeply attracted to him and feel he's pulling away, having sex will probably end the relationship. Communicate your boundaries around slowing down sexually, respecting your schedule, and calling earlier. If he does not step up, dump him. Don't project this one guy's bad behavior on all men. Someone else will treat you better.

Negative thought: I can't keep his attention. Guys want a supermodel and CEO of the Red Cross or some other charitable organization. I am not successful enough to find love.

Trigger: My guy friend is not interested in me even though we share emotional details about our lives.

Response: Ask guys what they want in a woman and they will usually say the same thing: attractive, successful, self-confident, and takes good care of herself. The problem is, in our girly heads, we can translate these to impossible standards if we aren't careful. Just because your guy friend can open up to you emotionally as you want a boyfriend to, it does not make him a good match for you. Love is like baking a cake, and it takes many ingredients. Although men will talk in generalities when describing their perfect girl, in reality, men's tastes vary dramatically. If a specific man has impossible standards, it is probably because he is afraid of intimacy. Do not project one person's opinion on all men.

Negative thought: I am too old. All the good ones are taken. I have missed my chance.

Trigger: I go out to functions with my girlfriends, but no one ever approaches us or asks me out. My younger, pretty, friend Susan is always going on dates. All my friends my age are either married or more bitter than I am about being single.

Response: You are too old for love only when you are dead! If you can breathe, you can find love. The fact that people are married means it is possible. Not everyone gets married at twenty-five, either. Some men need time to build their careers before they are ready to commit. Other men marry the wrong person and get divorced, before finding love.

They are wonderful prospects, as they enjoy being married, but just need to meet the right person. Often, the divorce matures them, especially if they were married for longer than ten years. If you are not being asked out at functions, then change the way you meet men. Try eHarmony or join church singles groups. Mix it up!

Negative thought: Everyone I know is married or in a relationship. Why not me? I have no one to go out with to find a man.

Trigger: When I see my friends, I am jealous of the couples in love and fear becoming the couple headed for divorce.

Response: It is very common to compare your love life to friends. Remember, however, your story is based on you. When you act in accordance with your feelings and values, you will live a happy life, regardless if you find a husband or not. If your friends seem wrapped-up in their own lives and don't have time to help you date, then go out and create your own life. You can join community groups, take a dance class for singles, or attend a lecture at a university. You can make new friends who will help you network and meet new people. Look at your friends' happy marriages and ask yourself, what can I learn or apply to my own dating strategy, based on their successes? You can also apply this thinking to those who failed. All represent opportunities to better understand yourself and what you want, not hold you back with fear, or shame you as a singleton.

Negative thought: I am not attractive. My friend Susan gets all the guys because she is so pretty. What do I have to offer?

Trigger: I look in the mirror and I don't think I am pretty.

Response: Ok, create a vision board for how you would like to look. Create a plan. Do you need to lose weight, get new clothes, or change your hair color? Are you neglecting yourself physically, and do you need to invest in self-care? Go to a department store and get a makeover for your wardrobe. Join www.bodybuilder.com or get a personal trainer. Or, maybe you just need to change your thinking. On 4x6 flashcards, write "I am beautiful, I enjoy the way my... (name three great things about your look). I also appreciate my... (name what you don't like about yourself, e.g., your legs), as it enables me to... (name the utility or purpose, e.g., legs enable me to run in the sun on a warm spring day). Say this to yourself while looking in the mirror everyday for a month. Just the act of trying is enough to build your self-confidence.

Negative thought: I am too fat to date. I need to lose 20+ lbs first.

Trigger: I weighed myself and I am clinically overweight.

Response: No matter how much you weigh, you cannot increase or decrease your self-worth. If you plan on sharing your life with someone, your weight will inevitably go up and down, and you need a husband who is mature enough to love you at any weight. Also, this was something my sister used to tell me all the time, that my weight was the main problem of why I had not found someone. One day I just yelled at her, "Fat people get married everyday! People in love who are not perfect. Probably more often than thin people, given our nation's weight statistics." The more accepting you are of yourself at any weight, the more accepting your partner will be, and the faster you will find love.

Negative thought: If I don't feel good about myself, how is someone else supposed to feel attracted to me?

Trigger: I rejected this guy who asked me out on a date because I am scared he will find out about my problems and run.

Response: Everyone has baggage. If you live on this earth, you are going to get banged up every once in awhile. The process of healing makes you better able to recognize emotions and deal with difficult life situations. Everyone fears rejection in dating, but rejection is God's protection. It prevents you from wasting all your time trying to get someone to love you who is incapable, for whatever reason. Instead, you move on to a relationship that is so much better, natural, and easy. Don't fixate on a guy; dedicate yourself to finding a husband, whoever that may be, and enjoy the adventure along the way.

Negative thought: I ruin every date by talking too much, taking control, or boring him to death.

Trigger: My last date has not called.

Response: You can only ruin what was not meant to be. When you meet the guy who is going to be your husband, you will feel at ease in your own skin and with your natural behaviors. That guy was not a match. Who cares? I can date someone else. There is not a big L for Loser on my forehead just because this guy did not find me appealing. It was just not meant to be.

Negative thought: I ruin every date by being quiet. I never have anything interesting to say, so I don't say anything at all.

Trigger: My last date has not called.

Response: You are interesting. If you breathe, you are special. Why? Because do you know what the odds are that you came into this world at all? How many eggs and sperm died before and after you were conceived, hoping to have a chance at creating life? Recognize how lucky you are to experience life. Instead of prejudging yourself or trying to determine the outcome of how someone feels about you, just stay open. If you did not feel like talking on your last date, who cares. Maybe he wasn't that "interesting", either. Try creating friendships with men through community services, political groups, or some common interests or values you share. In that way, you will have a lot to talk about instead of just sitting there.

Negative thought: I clam up inside when I really like someone, and then he is not interested in me.

Trigger: I was at a bar, and this guy came up to me, and I just froze up.

Response: Your expectations are too high. You have no idea who this guy is. Just because you have butterflies, does not mean he has relationship potential. He may be right for you, or he may not be. You just like the way he looks, but you need to gather more info before you decide to date him. Commit yourself to finding your husband; put him through the "Gauntlet" described in chapter 9.

Negative thought: I don't feel anything. I am not attracted to anyone.

Trigger: You just went on your fifth date with a guy who is nice, but you don't find him attractive.

Response: Healing takes time. In order to feel something for a man, you need to practice feeling in general. Practice reciprocity (as described in chapter 9) and pay attention to how you are feeling, I mean, any feeling, sad, angry, stomach upset, while you are on a date. If you keep trying, you will find the right guy. Maybe you are feeling nothing because he is not the right one, and that is ok, too.

You may be addicted to high drama or the need to feel intensity early on in a relationship. Although feeling butterflies is fun, the fundamental reason why people fall in love is that, over a period of time, the man consistently acts in ways of loving kindness toward you, and is emotionally open to you when you reciprocate. Keep trying, and you will grow in your ability to love, and then you will be ready when your husband comes along.

If you don't want to have sex with the man you are dating, than I would break up with him, as a romantic union includes sex, and dating someone you are not attracted to can be a way of avoiding real intimacy. Of course waiting to have sex until you are married is a great idea, but if you don't ever have an urge to be with him sexually then you should let him go. I am talking about feelings, not necessarily actions, when I make this point. If you never have feelings for any man you date, go see a medical doctor and get lab work done.

Negative thought: I can't stop thinking about "Joe." He is the only one for me.

Trigger: He didn't call you back, cheated on you, was violent, withdrew when you opened up emotionally, or exhibited any other form of rejection or abuse.

Response: The reason why you are attracted to him is because you believe he is the key to your feeling a certain way about yourself. He's not. Think about what you feel in his presence, and give that to yourself. Your husband will compliment what *you* have already created in your life.

Negative thought: I like bad boys. I don't feel intensity and emotion unless I am not sure where the relationship is headed.

Trigger: You date guys who are unavailable, such as married men, unemotional men, and men who run hot and cold in their intentions and feelings toward you.

Response: I used to really enjoy being pursued by an attractive, highly sexual man. I had this one boyfriend who bought me cards, jewelry, and lingerie within two months of dating me. It felt great to be wanted by someone so good- looking. I bet you can guess that it ended badly. Every woman wants to be wooed, but what you may not know is that good guys can woo, too. They may not invest in you, however, until a level of trust is built up between you. In other words, you can get the same intensity and sexual passion from a relationship that starts slow, if you are open to it and patient. Best of all, these relationships are more stable and often result in marriage.

Negative thought: I am attracted to men who are a challenge and "hard to get."

Trigger: You date only rich, good-looking, successful, type A men who have the nice house, car, boat, airplane, etc. They are aggressive in all aspects of their lives and only want the best. Their approval by asking you on a date means you are someone, too.

Response: Sometimes, hard-to-get men are assholes. Many women are willing to do anything to get them, and these men's egos prevent them from having realistic expectations from a relationship. I am not saying you should settle, but be open to love in the way the universe intends to deliver it to you. My husband is not rich; half his net worth was taken in his divorce. He is an engineering manager, not an investment banker. But I married him because I love who he is in the world: the way he tackles a problem; the way he looks at life; the kindness he displays to strangers; and most of all, the amazing way he loves me everyday. No amount of money compares to who he is. Be open to love in any form.

Negative thought: I need to feel sexually attracted to date someone. If I don't feel an instant click, I am not interested

Trigger: You reject 90 percent of the men who ask you out. You want your equal and nothing else.

Response: It is ok to have attraction high on the list of your needs in a relationship. It is not ok to use it as an impossible standard in order to reject any man who may potentially get close to you. Trust takes time. It is trust and not butterflies that long-term relationships are built on. Are you using this thought process as a way not to get hurt? That is, to reject them before they reject you?

Negative thought: My feelings are a roller-coaster. Sometimes I am really attracted to him, and other times I am not.

Trigger: He wore an outfit or said something that really turned me off.

Response: It is normal to not be in love constantly. Everyone wants that emotional rush, but the truth is, these feelings are governed by chemical processes in the brain, and those butterfly feelings last up to two years at best. Before you get depressed at hearing this, let me assure you that there are other hormones that kick in, but they are just not as strong. Love is a commitment you make everyday and not ruled by an occasional doubt or fear. You are meant to wax and wane in your emotions toward someone, like the tides going in and out. Fundamentally, you need to ask yourself, is this fear, or is this my reacting to something he specifically did that is not in line with my values? If it is just fear, then keep dating. If there is something you don't respect or could not accept long-term about him, then dump him. But make sure you are dumping him for lacking a value match with you, and not out of fear of intimacy.

Negative thought: What if I end up not liking him after ten years of marriage?

Trigger: He handled a situation on a date inappropriately.

Response: Maybe, maybe not? Who knows? Why don't you waste the next ten years worrying about this, so, in the off-chance it actually happens, you are prepared. Ok, that was extreme, but what I am saying is, *don't worry*. Instead of projecting a dating mistake your partner committed on a date as a doomed marriage, why don't you talk to him about what he did, instead? Ask him what his motivation was. Was that his intention? What could you two do differently to avoid the situation in the future? Long-term marriage is about communicating your bad feelings and working through them. Practice during dating enables you to hone these skills and fills you with confidence that you are marrying the right person.

Negative thought: I would die if I got raped again. I would kill someone who tried to rape me.

Trigger: You saw a movie that had extreme violence or rape scenes.

Response: It can be scary trying to date after an attack. You might have strong emotions that other people may not understand. My recommendation is to spend some time with a trained therapist and talk it out. When you do start dating again, only date nice guys. It is ok to reject a guy, cancel a date, meet guys with friends, or slow the whole process down until you feel comfortable.

Anger is also a healthy emotion and a sign of healing. I do not recommend violence, and if you are at that stage, please call a rape hotline, and you will be talked through extreme emotions. This, too, shall pass.

Negative thought: Everyone looks at me differently after I tell them about the attack.

Trigger: A guy friend calls a girl he is dating crazy with too much baggage.

Response: Being vulnerable, being not perfect, admitting that you are flawed and loving yourself in spite of it all is the greatest love of all-- sing it Whitney Houston! Ok, but seriously, no one would ever get married if being perfect was required. By the way, your husband will have something imperfect about him, too, that you will have to accept. Slowly open up over time, and you will learn who he is as a person. If he can't forgive you, then you don't want to live your life with someone who would judge you, anyway. When Aaron and I told each other the worst things we had ever done in our lives, it brought us closer together. I trust him with any and everything about me, especially the bad things.

Negative thought: I can't stop crying when someone I like touches me sexually.

Trigger: Your boyfriend kissed you, and you freak out and think about the attack.

Response: Yes, especially when you first start dating after an attack, you can get a flashback to the attack. If you are with a good man, go very slowly. This will lesson over time, as your mind remembers that sex is a good thing between people in love. It is important when you are having a flashback to tell yourself that you are safe and in good hands. It is ok to feel pain, but remember this is a very different situation. This can be especially healing when your boyfriend reaffirms your right to go slowly or stop when you feel uncomfortable.

Negative thought: I am damaged goods. I will never be normal again.

Trigger: You cry for no reason. You just feel awful about yourself, and you don't want to be around others.

Response: You are depressed. This is a chemical reaction in your brain. Go see a medical doctor, talk therapist, exercise, sleep, eat right, and you will feel good again. Most importantly, this negative thought is a lie. It is not permanent, no matter how strongly you feel it is the truth.

Negative thought: I am a loser.

Trigger: I disappointed my (fill in the blank) boss, parent, boyfriend, friend, myself, etc.

Response: Again, it is impossible to be a total loser. Think about it. You would have to fail at everything you do: sleeping, eating, walking, talking, going to work, listening, relating to others. Most of the time, you probably do things well or moderately well. Remember, all successful people suck at something! They just don't dwell on what they don't do well. They spend all their energy on what they want to achieve and create in the world. Are you a loser, or have you just been too frightened to explore who you are and what you want out of life? Have you doomed yourself to a life of pain just because you might be average on your first try at learning a new skill? Would you be this hard on your best friend?

Negative thought: Bad things keep happening to me. I am a magnet for evil. I can't protect myself.

Trigger: Another attack happened, or a highly intense situation occurred.

Response: As much as I would like to tell you that you are bulletproof, you are not. That being said, you don't have to be a repeat victim. This is where a trained therapist can really shine. You may be having trouble identifying unsafe situations (see chapter 9: "Identifying Bad Men"); testing your boundaries; experimenting with your sexuality inappropriately with bad men; or just having bad luck. The truth is, there are skill sets you can learn that will improve your life and greatly reduce your chances of another attack. Get a therapist trained in rape, contact RAINN, or go to a police station and ask for information on how to prevent an attack. Do something that strengthens your ability to fight back. Who says you can't behave or act differently in ways that would reduce your chances of being attacked? I am living proof that change is possible. Just keep trying.

Negative thought: I am not sane or healthy enough to be loved.

Trigger: I feel awful on dates.

Response: Sometimes, it is healthy to take a break from dating. There is nothing wrong with going slow. However, believing you are damaged does not improve your chances of getting healthy. This negative thought defeats you, as it both labels you a loser as well as zaps your motivation to heal and get better. Stay open to love. Imperfect people are the only people who get married because we are all imperfect people. Whatever high standard you have set for yourself, let go of it. The reverse of this faulty statement is impossible to define. When are you healthy enough to date? What yardstick would you use to measure that? Anytime you have a thought associated with "not good enough," ignore the thought, as it does nothing but shame you and impede you in meeting your goal of happiness and peace. Remember that accepting your imperfection is the bliss of life and the stepping stone to falling in love with another flawed individual.

What If It Doesn't Work?

If you follow this list and fail, in other words, if you are having trouble identifying the faulty logic in your thinking, or don't feel a sense of relief, then take this list to your therapist and go over it together. I guarantee that another person, especially a trained therapist, can identify holes in your negative-thought armor. If you are resisting doing this, either change therapists because you might be resisting because you don't trust your therapist, or just recognize that you are emotionally attached to your negative thoughts. I understand. For a period of time, I found it difficult to let go of my depression; it was like a warm blanket I clung to for comfort. You can't feel bad or be disappointed if you already are.

If you are depressed, I recommend seeing a medical doctor and getting exercise in addition to scheduling a therapist appointment to do this assignment together. If this seems overwhelming, then call a friend or family member to help you. At bare minimum, sing your happy song, like "Zip-a-Dee-Doo-Dah," and dance around your apartment for thirty minutes. Doing something active will help you stop your negative thinking.

If you are feeling incredibly sad and considering suicide, call 1-800-SUICIDE (1-800-784-2433) or 1-800-273-TALK (1-800-273-8255) -- or the deaf hotline at 1-800-4889. *No matter how hopeless or worthless you are feeling, it is not real.* It is an imbalance in your brain chemistry that will change if you resist the urge. These strong feelings will pass when you exercise and follow a program with a medical doctor and talk therapist.

You have the capacity to feel joy. I promise. Over ten shitty things happened to me in my life, but *I never* gave up. Above all else, I knew God had a plan for me. You are not meant to be abused. You were meant for a much greater purpose--hang in there! My life is so beautiful now, and so can yours be. I understand how real those negative thoughts can feel, but trust me, they are not permanent.

Chapter 8: Hyper-vigilant

One of the worst aspects of PTSD was that my hyper-vigilance lasted for years. Because I was attacked multiple times by multiple people, I had developed a strong negative thought pattern. "There is nothing I can do to protect myself," "The threats will keep coming," "I must stay on high alert at all times." This fear bled into all aspects of my life, including my relationships with my family and my ability to hold a job. I was absolutely miserable. The smallest of conflicts was World War III, and I overreacted to the smallest negative gestures or feedback. I was moody, touchy, reactive, and highly emotional. These thoughts of being constantly attacked also prevented me from finding my true love, because why in the hell would I be so selfish as to bring someone else I loved into this twisted, awful, world of pain I called my life.

Things changed. As I said before, it is almost impossible to find a statement or scenario that is always negative in this world. After my second session with my therapist Jennifer, she asked me a very important question, "What is your current level of fear? From one being the lowest to five being the highest, what do you feel right now?"

"Four." I remember thinking this was a healthy number, considering the reality of the number of attacks. Her answer surprised me, "We are going to try to take that down to a 2. How do you feel right now as I say that?"

In my head, I could not believe what she was saying. My chest clenched up, and I felt like either hitting her or running for the door. I slowly regained my breathing pattern. My fear had become my protector. I was constantly alert to what was going on around me and to what other people were doing or thinking. This threat level had worked for many years in preventing attacks, and I was terrified by just the mere prospect of letting down my guard. I had blamed myself and felt intense shame for not protecting myself enough, especially when I was younger.

Jennifer spoke again, "What we are going to do is replace your fear with healthy coping skills. Ironically, these skills will be more effective in protecting you than the fear. This will also enable you to relax and enjoy your life more. You can build trust with someone you are dating. Trust is essential for healthy love. This will enable you to meet your goal of getting married to someone you love and have strong feelings for."

My ability to trust men emotionally was limited because I was injured in a dating relationship where I loved my boyfriend. I associated the emotional part of a relationship with my most vulnerable part of the rape. Someone who I loved hurt me twice--physically through the rape itself, and emotionally through the betrayal of trust. I could not understand how he could commit such a violent act on someone he loved.

In the past, I never opened up to the people I dated, and therefore I never felt feelings for them. I dated people because we were a good intellectual match or because I found them attractive, but never both, and I never explored the emotional side of dating. By limiting the ways I felt attracted to a person, I controlled how quickly the relationship progressed and whether I would get hurt again. However, the end result was always the same: superficial relationships that were short-lived, combined with an overwhelming sense of hopelessness that I would never feel what I was supposed to feel to find my true love. I was damaged goods.

By taking down this wall of fear, I would be able to trust someone with both my good and bad feelings. If you can't communicate like this with your partner, then it is difficult to have a good marriage, let alone develop enough feelings to want to get married.

I realized that if I wanted a different result in dating, I had to try something different. As I mentioned before, I had to accept that my goal was not just to stop bad things from happening, but, instead, to learn what to do in the moment. Good and bad events happened everyday. I was so hyper-vigilant, that anything bad, even a negative comment about my work performance from my boss, felt like life or death. I was trying to control everything and everyone so that I could not get hurt. The energy it took to stop bad things from happening was overwhelming, because you can't stop bad things from happening. I was reinjuring myself, because I believed that if bad things were happening, it was because I was failing to protect myself. My self-esteem plummeted.

One of the first things Jennifer and I worked on when it came to coping skills were interactions with men at work. I had struggled with authority figures at work, both because I was overreacting to their feelings and actions, but also because I was choosing unstable work environments. I guess this was my form of testing my boundaries in an unhealthy way. As I became healthier, I chose work environments that were much more normal. I was no longer attracted to high-drama situations or intensity as a way to feel feelings.

Jennifer also taught me that if I am always focused on the outside world, then I can't feel. She challenged me to try to understand what I was feeling inside when a "bad" event at work occurred, instead of focusing 100 percent on the event or the feelings of my boss. By paying attention to my own feelings, I would naturally become less hyper-vigilant and also make better decisions. If my actions were based on my feelings and not my interpretations of the events or my boss, than I would naturally make better decisions that fell in line with my own value system. This is the reverse of date rape, where you give your entire body to the one you love and become numb, because you know this decision is against your values or desires. You are sacrificing yourself and not making decisions based on who you are.

If you are startled by the fact that I connected something as normal as work conflict with the violence of rape, then that is a good sign. Another common problem sexual abuse victims have is in understanding degrees of "bad." Everything is bad, very bad. This all-or-nothing viewpoint comes from the confusion so common in dealing with the aftermath of rape. Often, everything prior to the event seemed so normal that when you go back over it in your head, you wonder who to blame or how to prevent it in the future. You decide to be extra cautious in all aspects of your "normal" life, just to be on the safe side of preventing another attack. This is the essence of hyper-vigilance. Nothing seems "normal" again.

Jennifer and I met weekly, and we reviewed all the bad events that occurred, no matter how normal they might have been. We discussed whether I was paying attention to my feelings in the moment and developing solutions based on who I was and my value system. At first I resisted this. I viewed it as selfish. I also thought it would not work, because if I got what I wanted, how were other people going to be ok with that. Surely my boss's opinion mattered more than my own. Again, this goes back to the fact that in a rape, someone overpowered you and got what they wanted. You had no choice. Your desires were not considered.

Jennifer convinced me that if a bad event occurred that it did not matter. Whatever happened, if I were true to my feelings and value system, then I would get what I wanted. For example, let's say my boss dislikes me. I mean really dislikes me, and it wasn't just my overreacting to a negative comment. He is out to get me and wants to fire me. He orchestrates a series of events and goals and makes it impossible for me to achieve them. (Notice how rape victims are extremely sensitive to a loss of control, injustice, or being overpowered.)

Instead of agreeing with the tragedy and hopelessness of the situation, I can feel something. I can feel that my boss is an ass. I can feel that I am not in a stable environment. Then I can say, "Well who cares if I lose this awful job anyway? I can start looking for a job now with a company that better matches my values. I can put my energy into building a resume, interviewing, and knowing that very soon I will be in a better place. I will do the bare minimum at work, because do I really care about pleasing a narcissistic boss?"

I do not have to associate myself with the boss nor feel controlled or victimized by him, and that is exactly what would happen if I stayed hyper-vigilant, trying to prevent a bad thing from happening. In fact, if I concentrated on his feelings and the bad event of being fired, I would miss out on all the good things that could come from getting a new job: better pay, a better position, and a more stable work environment.

The more you concentrate on how you are feeling and what your values are, instead of trying to prevent things from happening, the happier you will be. The bad event or person will immediately have less power over you. Your creative power to solve problems and create a better life for yourself will improve your self-esteem and self-confidence. Others will notice this resilience in you, and your power base will grow. You will also appear less needy and controlling in relationships, and people will be drawn to you in friendships and in dating. This is God's way of turning shit into roses.

Another way to look at bad events is through the lens of time. In a year from now, are you going to care about this crappy boss? If you answered yes, than you are definitely hyper-vigilant. In reality, you keep in contact with those who love you. Think about it. As you move through life, your friends stay, and those you had conflict with naturally slip out of your everyday life. I bet you may still keep in contact with a high school friend, but I bet you never have dinner with your awful, sophomore Spanish teacher who humiliated you in front of the class when you could not pronounce "vaca." The point is that you only keep the bad people around in your mind, not in your physical presence. Therefore, you have total control over how long you intend to stay in pain because of a bad event or person. My advice is to clear out those memories by debunking your negative thoughts.

Remember, it is not the bad event itself but the meaning you assign to it that negatively affects you. Notice how I could have assigned the meaning that I was a no good, horrible employee to the boss's actions of trying to destroy my career. I might have gone on to think that I was incapable of pleasing a boss or holding down a job. As a result, I would not have been able to support myself as an adult and I would have become homeless or had to move back in with my parents. I might have further indulged these depressed thoughts by believing this meant I was a worthless human being who would always suffer. No wonder I am sad. Do you think interviewing for a job with all these negative thoughts in my head is going to get me to a better next step in my career? Or maybe this lack of self-esteem would put me in an even worse, more unstable environment, as I desperately take any opportunity, thus creating a self-fulfilling prophecy.

Notice how all this could be avoided by starting with yourself and what is best for you. It is not selfish; it is how you love and honor yourself by putting your needs first. It is also how you form your sense of self. You let people know who you are in the world by telling them what you do and don't want. If they react negatively, you do not take that on as part of yourself, but instead see them as a separate entity responsible for getting their own needs met. My boss wanted a new employee. I wanted a better job. We can both get what we want. Win--win.

If you take this thought process one step further, you will notice that maybe there is no value in labeling events or people as good or bad. It is as if you are creating two problems for yourself: first, the challenge that life presents; and second, the fear of what the event means. What would happen if you held off on assigning meaning to the event and went straight to figuring out what is the optimal solution for you, without judging or labeling yourself or those involved? It might make the bad man less scary or the challenge less steep.

Fear can paralyze you from taking healthy, corrective action. It might also act like distorting glasses, magnifying how bad things are or discounting your ability to handle the situation effectively. You should not try to avoid fear altogether. Instead, thank fear and talk to it like a small child. It is ok that you fear this, but we can make it through this storm. Thanks for alerting me something is wrong, but I can take care of it. In *Calling in the One* by Katherine Woodward Thomas, there is a wonderful exercise about how to deal with fear on page 256. I highly recommend it.

Chapter 9: Lower Your Guard Without Being Vulnerable in Dating

The next thing Jennifer and I worked on was a plan for dating. The first and hardest thing I had to do was believe that a man who could fulfill my desires existed. In a world of six billion people, I strongly believed that there was not a man out there who was kind, intelligent, handsome, and most of all, trustworthy.   And if he did exist, he would not find me attractive or love me back.   If you have not guessed already, this is a depressed thought. Anything that is an overgeneralization with a 100 percent negative outcome rarely, if ever, exists in nature.

In sessions, Jennifer constantly challenged this negative belief that my husband did not exist. Just believe it is possible. If you believe, you will make better choices in whom you choose to date. Just as in picking a job, you will choose better if you think something better is out there and you are capable of achieving it. The day I fully embraced that he existed, is the day love came into my life. No, I did not go on a date with my husband the next day, but my heart had changed. I was finally open for love. The world seemed lighter, more colorful. I was filled with anticipation about meeting him. Would I meet him tomorrow? Maybe. It was now possible.

Healthy relationships start small with casual encounters. This is the opposite expectation that someone has after being raped: all encounters are full of high drama. Just as in the job scenario, in a dating situation, if you are concentrating on your date's feelings and preventing something bad from happening, then you are missing out on understanding your own feelings and making decisions that match your value system. Ironically, pay less attention to him and more attention to how you feel when you are with him. This will help you connect with your feelings, and love will grow in your heart, if he is a good person and match for you. If you are focused on him, his reactions to you, or preventing a break-up or the possibility of getting hurt again, then you will appear needy, controlling, "off," and the relationship will slip through your fingers.

Healthy men love women with standards. They respect boundaries. They need to know you are a fully formed women with ideas and principles before they can trust and fall in love with you. If you just give them what they want without considering your own desires and values, you are not being unselfish, you are being stupid. The negative aspects of you are still you. No is not rejection. It is insight into who you are. A good man will respect "no." Even if it is "no, I do not like that restaurant," start telling people who you are today.

Identifying Attackers

When I first started seeing Jennifer I asked her if I should stop dating men while I am trying to heal from the past. Her answer surprised me, "No, I think it is a good idea for you to continue dating. As you date, we can identify patterns that are holding you back. We can also discuss the quality of men you are selecting as dating partners."

Ironically, when you start dating again, you may be more tolerant of bad behaviors in men. But, the more accepting you are of these bad behaviors, the more your self-esteem plummets. This is why it is important to be in touch with your feelings when you date, so that you can identify bad men and weed them out quickly.

Before every attack, there is usually a moment when the attacker tests his opportunity with the victim. I call this the shark bump. Just as a shark knocks its prey first before eating it, sexual predators test boundaries. The most important thing is to respond immediately. When I had my massage, my therapist got a little too close to my upper, inner thigh before the attack happened. I could have told him that I did not want to be touched inappropriately or ended the massage right then. My intuition was telling me something was wrong, but I ignored it. I am not accepting responsibility for this person's actions, but setting boundaries is a good way of preventing attacks. When you don't go numb, stay in contact with your body and feelings, you will act to protect yourself.

Later on in my life, I went to another massage therapist on a recommendation of a friend. This therapist had worked with a doctor, so I felt safe. After our first session, I was suspicion, because the massage therapist had given me a two-hour massage and charged me for one hour. Before our next massage, I explained to him that I never want to be touched in an inappropriate manner. I looked him straight in the eye. He agreed and said he would never do such a thing. He honored that promise with me.

A few months later, my friend calls me, apologizing, and saying I need to call the police. I asked her why, and she said that the massage therapist she recommended was being charged with rape and sexual abuse. He videotaped having sex with his clients, and his wife found the videos on his computer. Multiple clients had stepped forward, and the police were collecting statements. Although being this close to another sexual predator scared the hell out of me, I also felt proud that I had set my boundaries and I was not abused. Never underestimate how powerful it is to look someone in the eye and say, "No!"

The Gauntlet--My Process for Choosing a Healthy Relationship

Over the next few months, I embraced these principals and formed my dating plan with Jennifer. I fondly refer to it as "The Gauntlet." Because it can be challenging for someone who has experienced trauma to engage in casual conversation and date at a slow pace, begin by viewing your dating life as a test that a man must pass, that is, he must attempt to get through a gauntlet to win your heart. He has to pass through a series of steps before you reach intimacy or engage in heavy conversation. If he gets knocked off the gauntlet before getting to the end where you open up your heart to him, then he was not meant to be. He is not your husband.

The first step is small. Dinner, or perhaps even a daytime activity, such as going for a coffee or a walk around the park. As much as you can, have few expectations for this first date when it comes to feeling emotion for this man. The first date is about seeing if he would make a nice friend. If your heart skips a beat, great, but remember, if you don't have strong feelings at first, it does not mean that you won't develop feelings in the future. You have time. He has to make it through the gauntlet first before you open your heart. Start small. Most of all, you are observing if his patterns of behavior honor you, and then you can reciprocate.

I am a huge supporter of woman's rights, but the next few lines may seem that I am more Victorian in my dating advice. The reason why I make these recommendations, however, is because they protect you and they work. Bear with me, and you will see that I am not telling you to act in a certain way and then he will like you, or that you must be submissive. Not at all. I am just advising you to keep the upper hand at all times. You are the decider, not the doer. He has to run the gauntlet. Don't try to meet him halfway or help him. You want to make sure that you are actively making the decision to date him and not reacting out of fear of rejection. Helping him through the gauntlet means you either fear your husband does not exist, therefore "I will settle for less than my standards," or that you desperately want to feel something with someone, even if it is short-lived. Don't help him. It ruins your self-esteem. Besides, you will respect him more if he survives to win your heart.

Reciprocation is the safe way to let down your wall of fear and build trust in a relationship without being vulnerable. He does something nice, you do something nice back. He opens up about something personal, you open up about something personal. He calls you on the phone, you call him back.

Here is the Victorian advice--*he* has to initiate the activity. What about the modern woman? Why can't I just go after what I want and lead the conversation? Or ask him out on a date? Because when you are doing, you are not deciding. Your job is to watch him to ensure that when he acts and does something, you feel good about it, and it fits with your value system. You are not trying to control him or the outcome, but, instead, you should be observing, feeling, and deciding whether this is what you want. It does not matter if he likes you. What matters is if you like him. If you make the first move, you are trying to control things and you will get lost in your feelings. Your ego will be wrapped-up around getting rejected. By waiting for him to make the first move, second move, and so on, you are watching him successfully navigate the gauntlet to win your heart. He runs the gauntlet, not you.

This is the best time to review your dating activity with your therapist to ensure that your intuition of whether your date is a good person or not is accurate. If the man is moving very fast sexually, although that may feel validating and intense, he may not be interested in you in the long run. Explain that you want him to slow down, and if he doesn't, he failed the gauntlet. The man may be flighty or inconsiderate. He may call you late at night or make plans at the last minute. If you like him, tell him nicely that you don't date men who call you at the last minute, and you would appreciate more notice. If he does not change, then he failed the gauntlet.

I highly recommend, when giving men negative feedback, to phrase it in such a way that it is your standard or dating rule based on past experiences. Then it is no longer about him, but what you are willing or unwilling to put up with. You are setting a boundary that is not up for discussion. Some men will try to test these boundaries or make you feel as if you don't deserve this treatment. They just failed the gauntlet. The person who is going to be your husband will always try to raise your self-esteem, not make you feel less than.

Many men failed the gauntlet before I met Aaron. Aaron sailed right through easily, naturally. Women who have good relationships with their husbands will usually tell you two things about dating their husbands before they were married. It was easy, and he was so nice to me I knew he was different. Men who want to marry you and are worthy of marriage treat you well. They do what they say they are going to do. They respect you. They are not in a hurry to get somewhere either sexually or emotionally. They earn the right to become your best friend over time and with constant, good behavior.

Table 2: Unhealthy men versus healthy men

Unhealthy men	Healthy men
Flighty, inconsistent--he	*Consistent, focused–*

doesn't call when he says he will call. He asks you out at the last minute. He sometimes waits several weeks before asking you out again. You question whether or not he really likes you.	he asks you out soon after the last date, calls ahead to schedule time with you on the weekends. He values your time. You know he likes you.
Untrustworthy–what he says and what he does are not the same. He has done something that goes against your value system to another person in the past. He may brag about treating someone else badly, such as an ex-girlfriend, but claims things will be different with you. He says he believes in something, but you observe him doing something to the contrary. He tries to get you to do things to please him that are contrary to your value system: move too fast sexually, put up with bad behavior, etc.	*Trustworthy*–what he says and what he does are the same. He is authentic. You feel safe in his presence. He actively pursues you in a respectful manner. His action and words match up with your value system. You respect who he is in the world. He honors you with his actions.

Emotionally immature– he withdraws when you share something emotional. He dislikes negative conversations about changing his behaviors or when you inform him of a boundary. He has difficulty communicating his emotions or problem solving. He erupts in anger at minor frustrations in life. He withdraws during discussions about the relationship or where you are headed. He likes leaving you in suspense about his feelings and intentions.	Emotionally mature– he wants to know more about you, including your wants, desires, likes, and dislikes. When you inform him of a boundary, he immediately corrects or explains why he acts the way he does and searches for a fair and reasonable compromise. He is level-headed and faces life's challenges without anger. He can feel emotion without being scared of it, including the feeling of love and wanting to commit his life to you.
Relationship nightmare– he has few friends who he shares true intimacy or deep conversations with. He can either have no friends or everyone is his friend and therefore has no intimacy. He is mean to strangers or	Relationship savvy–he has long-term, deep connections with several friends. He treats people with kindness and respect. He likes his family (it is ok to have a conflict with some members

service staff like waiters or waitresses, as if he is better than they are. His relationship with his family is strained. He intensely dislikes his mother or authority figures. He has trouble keeping a job or staying committed to anything longer than two years. He has trouble relating to your friends and family.	of the family, but if he doesn't have a good reason why there is a strain in the relationship, this could be a red flag). He gets along with your friends and family.
Intense at first, then withdraws—he pursues you aggressively in the first month, wanting to spend all his time with you. He wants to move fast sexually, and tempts you to go faster than your pace. When you open up about emotions or your intentions, he withdraws.	*Slow at first, but always interested*--he enjoys just hanging out with you, getting to know you. He shares stories about his life and who he is. He has goals, and marriage is one of them. He makes sure you feel good and are taken care of. He anticipates your needs. He is thoughtful when you open up emotionally.
Controlling and	*Accepting*—he sees

Manipulative–he wants *all* of your time and is jealous of other close relationships you may have with friends and family. He speaks poorly of your friends and family in attempts to isolate you from other people. He is irrationally jealous of other men like guy friends or coworkers. He may erupt in anger and accuse you of cheating or encouraging sexual advances from other men. He controls what you wear in public and degrades you if you *look* to sexy. He expects you to check in with him all the time and you must respond by phone or text immediately when he contacts you. When he is angry or irrational, he blames it on your behavior.

your friends and family as an extension of you and honors them with his actions and words. He encourages you to spend time with them. He is not jealous of acquaintances or friendships with other men. He enjoys your sexuality and your style of dress. You don't have to check in with him or be available to him 24 hours a day. He takes responsibility for his emotions and actions, and apologizes if he makes mistakes. He does not blame you for his bad behavior.

Sex Before Love

Although high-intensity trysts with a good-looking guy may seem like a fun way to get your needs met before meeting your husband, it pales in comparison to the love you experience in a healthy relationship. Intimacy is not sex. Sex does not define how well the relationship is going. Sex is always second to trust. If not, the relationship explodes. Trust is love, and it takes time and continual interactions to develop.

I used to avoid sex as a coping mechanism, and then when I finally found someone to date, I raced to sex and wanted it often. Jennifer was puzzled and wanted to know why I was hung-up on sex and often probed my motivation. It was because, to me, the ability to finally feel comfortable enough to have sex meant that I was experiencing love. I was starving for love and connection. The problem is that sex is sex. Trust is love. You can have sex at any time in a relationship. You have to wait patiently for trust to develop, and you can't control it or make it happen. It just is.

When you give up control of the outcome of a relationship, you start experiencing more meaningful relationships when you act in accordance with your values and feelings. Not all men will survive the gauntlet. Some may survive the gauntlet and be worthy of trust but not be the right one for you. Finally, one day, a man will make it through and love you. Trust me, he is worth the wait!

Final Thoughts

"There is no end to new beginnings!" -Alfonso
Avagliano

Changing your frame of mind to be open to intimacy is a process. The gauntlet helps protect you along the way. Eventually, you will achieve the ultimate goal of trusting and loving yourself. When you are aware of your feelings and acting in accordance with your values, you will see the fruitful outcomes of your decisions. You have aligned *who you are* with how you react to life's challenges instead of acting out of fear.

I wish you great success in finding and marrying the man of your dreams. I also wish you the simple joy of everyday life as you move from hyper-vigilant to an acceptance of good and bad in the world and a confidence in your ability to meet those challenges. But most of all, I wish you peace and a moment of silence from your negative thoughts. I wish you the joy of feeling good in your own skin again and the confidence in the direction your life is headed. I see your rose garden blooming.

On your way to happiness, this summarizing chart will help you gauge your progress in your recovery.

Table 3: Healing chart: unhealthy versus healthy thoughts and actions

Unhealthy thoughts and actions	Healthy thoughts and actions
Putting all your energy and effort into stopping bad things from happening in your life.	Trusting your ability to make good decisions and take actions based on your values and goals when a problem arises.
Overreacting to a failed event and inappropriately taking responsibility.	Separating yourself from the event or failure. Not overgeneralizing the failure as a judgment on your self-worth. Recognizing it as an opportunity for growth.
Solving other people's problems for them, including authority figures.	Allowing others to fail and recognizing this as a growth opportunity for them. Not feeling responsible for solving things when the time and effort would compromise your goals

	or values. Seeing yourself as separate from others and their failures.
Overreacting to other people's negative emotions. Absorbing those emotions as your own, or compromising your values and happiness to meet their needs above your own. Going numb.	Allowing someone to be emotional in your presence and remaining calm. Setting your boundaries and not swaying from your values. Being ok with disappointing or angering someone else.
Labeling yourself as a failure, not good enough. Overgeneralizing when bad things happen.	Looking at the specifics of a situation and creating practical solutions. Seeing the problem from multiple perspectives.
Highly sensitive to criticism. Feeling overpowered or helpless. Feeling incapable of change.	Looking for truth in the criticism and what value you can gain from it in enhancing your life and achieving your goals. Separating the emotion of feeling rejected from your sense of self. Recognizing the value

	of learning from feedback, and being ok with dismissing the criticism if it is not in line with your values.
Unrealistic expectation of outcomes, other people, or self. Needing things to be perfect before you can relax and be happy.	Enjoying life as an adventure, accepting the natural ups-and-downs. Appreciating times of accomplishment and love, and learning from times of struggle. Feeling happy regardless of outside stimulus. Self-esteem is based on consistently making decisions in line with values and goals.
Letting your guard down to strangers or inappropriately in dating situations. Using emotionally charged stories about attacks to create intimacy too quickly.	Carefully choosing who to open up to about past events. Being satisfied with everyday interactions and not feeling the need to speed things up when initially getting to know someone.
Using sex to create intimacy.	Dating understanding reciprocity. Ensuring

	partner has emotional maturity, values, and life goals before opening up to sex. Recognizing sex is not intimacy. Trust is. And it takes time to develop.
Using the attack as a way to reject dates. Saying you are not ready versus being honest about your level of attraction for the other person.	Being honest with dating partners about what you want and don't want. Ending relationships that are unhealthy or not what you want.
Keeping bad people in your life to make things right or refusing to accept what happened.	Carefully choosing who you allow in your inner circle. Selecting friends and dates based on values matches. Releasing the need to fix a bad relationship.
Keeping bad people in your head.	Releasing the words and events of people who do not support or help you grow. Talking back to any generalizations or negative thoughts you have acquired from these people.

Feeling overwhelmed.	Taking healing in bite-size chunks. Honoring your efforts in the mirror. Acting in loving kindness as you grow and take chances in life.
Drinking alcohol, eating unhealthy foods, not getting eight hours sleep, not exercising, gaining weight to avoid being raped.	Taking loving care of your body. Putting your health first. Being in your body and feeling emotion and feelings.
Taking risky chances or tempting fate as an effort to control and prevent bad things from happening.	Accepting what happened.
Being on high alert at all times for the next attack.	Recognizing that you are vulnerable, as are all humans. Fear is not the best protection. The solution is to use both your logical and emotional brain to solve problems and make decisions.

If you enjoyed this book, I would greatly appreciate a book review on Amazon. If you did not enjoy it, you probably did not get to this part. ☐

Resources

Author's website: www.datingaftertrauma.com

Check out my website for speaking engagements, my blog, and other helpful tips. I would greatly appreciate hearing about your progress in healing.

Sexual Abuse & Rape:

National Sexual Assault Hotline at 1.800.656.HOPE (4673).

RAINN – Rape, Abuse, and Incest National Network , http://www.rainn.org/

Safe Place – Ending Sexual and Domestic Violence, http://www.safeplace.org/, 24 hour hotline: 512-267-SAFE or 927-961-6TTY

Depression:

Call 1-800-SUICIDE (1-800-784-2433) or 1-800-273-TALK (1-800-273-8255)--or the deaf hotline at

1-800-4889

http://www.livestrong.com/depression/

http://www.webmd.com/depression/default.htm

http://www.mayoclinic.com/health/depression/DS0 0175

Post Traumatic Stress Disorder:

http://www.livestrong.com/ptsd/

http://www.mayoclinic.com/health/post-traumatic-stress-disorder/DS00246

Other books I recommend:

Calling in the One by Katherine Woodward Thomas, copyright 2004, ISBN 1-4000-4929-6

Feeling Good by Dr. David D. Burns, copyright 1999, ISBN 978-0-380-81033-8

Made in the USA
Monee, IL
17 April 2020